What People Are Saying about Dr. Joseph Ripley and *Life to the Fullest*...

This book provides practical understanding that will annihilate once and for all the strongholds that attempt to permeate your life! It is God's will for you to be reconciled with Him and enjoy His presence. If you have met with obstacles when trying to avoid the words of those who contradict the promises of God for your life, make this book a part of your permanent library. Now is the time to break the insanity cycles that operate in your life by doing something different and expecting different results!

—Creflo Dollar
Founder and Senior Pastor, World Changers Church International

I encourage you to make *Life to the Fullest* part of your personal library. Through Dr. Ripley, God will show you how to change your thinking, how to get over excuses and overcome your past, and how, when you fail, He engineers a comeback on your behalf. Read it and reread it. Give a copy to your friends—saved and unsaved. Strike out against fear and walk in the fullness of a life lived deliberately and to the glory of God.

—Bishop Eddie L. Long
Pastor, New Birth Missionary Baptist Church, Lithonia, Georgia
Founder and CEO, New Birth Christian Academy
Author, It's Your Time *and* The Elect Lady

Sit down and enjoy yourself, because this is a good read. It will not only bless you and minister life to you, but it will also cause spiritual nutrition to come into your spirit, into your soul, and into your body. Enjoy *Life to the Fullest*. I sure did!

—Dr. Jesse Duplantis
Founder, Jesse Duplantis Ministries

In my life, I want to be the same kind of servant and love people the way that Dr. Joe Ripley and his wife, Marjanita, love me and other people. He has got to be one of God's chosen pastors, and I know that God is proud of him, his wife, and his family for the work they are doing for the Lord.

—Dr. Norvel Hayes
Founder and President, Norvel Hayes Ministries
Founder, New Life Bible College, Cleveland, Tennessee
Founder and President, New Life Maternity Home

This book will help you discover how to live the abundant life you have desired and that God has promised you in His Word. I encourage you to take the time to read these pages and let them inspire you to live each day as a champion for God.

—Reverend Kenneth W. Hagin
President, Kenneth Hagin Ministries
Senior Pastor, RHEMA Bible Church

Life to the Fullest may be the template you need to duplicate the model of wholeness he exemplifies in every arena. Now is a time when all of us need the wisdom he shares to have the abundant life the Scriptures promise the believer. If I were you, I would give it a read!

—Bishop T. D. Jakes
Senior Pastor, The Potter's House, Dallas, Texas

The principles and strategies in this book are life changing. If you desire to live your life to its fullest, read this book now.

—Bob Harrison
America's Increase Activist
Best-selling author

Pastor Ripley is truly a man of God. Over the last twenty-three years, he has been my friend, spiritual mentor, and a blessing to me and my family. Thank you for the dynamic and encouraging chapel services before my games. They gave me the strength to win. I know this book will inspire many to live *Life to the Fullest*!

—Kevin Willis
NBA Champion San Antonio Spurs
CEO, Walker & Willis Clothing

Dr. Ripley has been a loyal and constant supporter and life coach. His wisdom and insight have helped me overcome and triumph over many of the pressures and challenges professional athletes face. I strongly believe that everyone who reads this book, and purposes to incorporate in their lives the insights he shares, will be better for it!

—Ovie Mughelli
NFL Atlanta Falcons
Founder, The Ovie Mughelli Foundation

LIFE
to the
FULLEST

LIFE
to the
FULLEST

Soaring to Purposeful Living

DR. JOSEPH RIPLEY

WHITAKER
HOUSE

LIFE TO THE FULLEST
Soaring to Purposeful Living

Dr. Joseph Ripley
The Body of Christ Church International, USA
P.O. Box 490346
College Park, Georgia 30349
www.bocciusa.com

ISBN: 978-1-60374-100-2
Printed in the United States of America
© 2009 by Joseph Ripley

Whitaker House
1030 Hunt Valley Circle
New Kensington, PA 15068
www.whitakerhouse.com

Library of Congress Cataloging-in-Publication Data

Ripley, Joseph, 1954–
  Life to the fullest / by Joseph Ripley.
    p. cm.
  Summary: "Uses Scripture passages and biblical examples to teach Christians to see themselves the way God sees them—as overcomers—and equips them to defeat their fears, build courage, and live in victory"—Provided by publisher.
  Includes bibliographical references (p.   ).
  ISBN 978-1-60374-100-2 (trade pbk. : alk. paper) 1. Success—Religious aspects—Christianity. I. Title.

BV4598.3.R56 2009
248.4—dc22
                      2008053912

1 2 3 4 5 6 7 8 9 10 11 12 **W** 16 15 14 13 12 11 10 09

Foreword

When I learned that Dr. Ripley was writing a book about changing wrong directions to right ones and bad circumstances to a point of victory, I was enthralled!

Anyone who knows me knows I am an advocate for change. Change is the inevitable component of fulfillment in our lives. It takes change in order to experience the fullness of God when we operate outside His will. My first thought was, *My God, Dr. Ripley is on to something!* This is not only a good word for such a time as this, it is a ***now*** Word, for real-life situations and people seeking real answers.

To the casual reader, this book may appear to be like any other self-help book. I assure you—it is not! One of the things that stood out for me was Dr. Ripley's unique way of presenting how to use the power of your imagination to go from where you are now to where God wants you to be. No matter what your physical eyes may see, your spiritual eyes see the truth of God's Word above mere facts that try to discredit it.

I know Dr. Ripley personally; in fact, as often as we can, we get together for lunch and fellowship. He is a true Word-seeker. Unlike many others, whose edification may come from one-day-per-week church attendance, Dr. Ripley lives, eats, and breathes the Word of God! I know him to be a high achiever, strong believer, and advocate for overcoming through God's Word. We as believers are *predestined* to be overcomers. If there are areas of your life where you fall short, pick up a copy of this book right away and take advantage of the practical insights God provides through Dr. Ripley to experience *right-now* change!

This book provides practical understanding that will annihilate once and for all the strongholds that attempt to permeate your life! It is God's will for you to be reconciled with Him and enjoy His presence. If you have met with obstacles when trying to avoid the words of those who contradict the promises of God for your life, make this book a part of your permanent library. Now is the time to break the insanity cycles that operate in your life by doing something different and expecting different results!

—*Creflo Dollar*
Founder and Senior Pastor, World Changers Church International

Contents

Introduction

God wants you to succeed in life. It's been established in His economy from the very beginning. This truth means that wherever you are right now, you can change your direction, you can change your circumstances, and you can change your life.

I realize that there are many hardships that happen to people and hinder some from changing their lives. You may take a look at your own life and think, *There's no way! I could never get past this problem or put this hardship behind me!* While it may be a fact that you aren't capable of overcoming, the truth is that you were created to be an overcomer— with the infinite ability and all-sufficiency of the God who created you because He lives inside you.

God loves you enough to walk right in through the front door of your life (through this book, at the moment), and say, "Look, I know what hurts you. I know what's ailing you. I am familiar with the issues in your life, and I know how to deliver you from them. In fact, I have delivered you from them. What I want to do now is convince you that your deliverance is complete. I will do this by bringing the truth to you. And the truth that you know, that you become intimate with, will make you free." (See John 8:32.)

I believe that God has revealed to me certain insights about this truth, as well as how to overcome life's obstacles, and I feel privileged to share these insights with you.

You know what it took to get to where you are. But do you know what it's going to take to get where you really want to go? Do you know what it will take to do what you really want to do? And do you know what God wants you to do?

We will explore these questions in this book, along with related issues—concepts such as self-image, thought life, whom and what you are listening to, the importance of seeing yourself from God's perspective, and dealing with fear.

A grave and dangerous threat to overcomers is the spirit of fear. *Most of what you must overcome has been brought on by fear.* I realize that this statement may seem shocking to you, but the truth is that if you're not careful or wary of fear, it may influence, control, and ultimately incapacitate you.

Debilitating fear is something that we can all live without. The apostle Paul declared, *"For God did not give us a spirit of timidity (of cowardice, of craven and cringing and fawning fear), but [He has given us a spirit] of power and of love and of calm and well-balanced mind and discipline and self-control"* (2 Timothy 1:7 AMP).

Fear can be described as an overwhelming emotion caused by real or imagined danger. Contrary to what many people believe, most fears are learned. This is a specific aspect of fear that we will discuss in greater detail. Some people would argue that they were born timid or shy, but fear is not a personality type. Timidity and cowardice are not character traits inherent at birth. They are temperaments that are developed in an individual as he or she grows up.

We can see in the above passage that any type of paranoid fear or timidity did not come from God.

CHANGING DIRECTION

There was a short period of time on the earth when fear did not dominate anyone. That was in the garden of Eden, before Adam or Eve ate of the forbidden fruit. Before the fall, they freely walked and talked with God in the cool of the day.[1] Then, fear appeared on earth for the first time after Adam fell through disobedience.

From that moment on, fear invaded the lives of all mankind. The first mention of fear in the Bible is found in Adam's excuse for hiding from God after he and Eve had sinned by eating of the forbidden fruit, realized that they were naked, and made coverings for themselves. When God summoned them, Adam answered, *"I heard thy voice in the garden, and I was afraid, because I was naked; and I hid myself"* (Genesis 3:10). From generation to generation, many people—young and old, rich and poor—have been dominated by fear. As a result, for these individuals, scores of dreams and desires were never fulfilled, success was never within reach, and the overcoming life was inaccessible, blocked by their own fears.

In this book, I want to show you how to loose yourself from whatever has been holding you back and to go on to fulfill your God-given destiny of living successfully.

For instance, you will learn that to overcome any fear, you first must change the way you think. In addition, you must be willing to go against the flow—which can feel as if you're swimming upstream against the current—to accomplish your dreams. Facing a fear may appear to others as going against conventional wisdom, and they will likely question you.

To overcome any fear, you first must change the way you think.

This includes the people who will tell you every reason why you cannot succeed. While they may genuinely care for your well-being, their words of "wisdom" will keep you bound in the fears that have constantly held you back.

You must determine in your heart not to listen to the naysayers who cross your path. Keep in mind that you will probably encounter more people who believe you will fail than people who will encourage you to cast off fear and tenaciously pursue everything God has for you.

I wrote this book to encourage you and to let you know that God wants you to live a full, meaningful, purposeful life—and that you have what it takes to do it.

The Scripture verses you read in these pages will be a great source from which you will draw the strength and courage needed to persevere in facing down whatever you want to overcome. Perseverance is among the greatest assets needed to defeat fear and be an overcomer in life. Here are other assets that will be covered in this book:

- Knowledge of the Scripture by reading, studying, and meditating upon it daily.

- Consistency in prayer: praying regularly in the Spirit[2] and in your native tongue.

- Faith: confessing, or affirming with the same words, what the Word of God says about you as God's own.

- Obedience to the Lord.

A crucial step to living victoriously as an overcomer is developing a working knowledge of the principles of the kingdom of God in order to assure that you fulfill His purposes for your life. Thus, we will constantly heed scriptural truths and biblical concepts throughout this book.

One thing is certain: if you continue doing what you have always done, you will remain exactly where you are right now.

One thing is certain: if you continue doing what you have always done, you will remain exactly where you are right now. My desire is to motivate, encourage, and enable you to challenge the fears and insecurities that are holding you back. With dogged determination, unwavering fortitude, and ironclad tenacity, you can reach a place where you are able to succeed, increase, and multiply.

It may seem difficult now, but I believe that once empowered by this message, you will realize that when God is with you, fear cannot stop you. You can overcome your fears, change your direction, and walk down the pathway of fear-free living to reach a destination of true success.

Chapter 1

You Are an Overcomer!

We can learn a valuable lesson about the tenacity to overcome by looking at the common salmon. These fish are born in fresh water, yet they later migrate to the ocean, where they live until they are ready to reproduce. After they have matured and are ready to spawn, they return to fresh water. Folklore has it that salmon go back to their birthplaces to lay their eggs.

Their journey is long and arduous. Once the Pacific salmon reach freshwater rivers and streams, they typically travel approximately nine hundred miles, swimming against rushing rapids, fighting strong currents, and climbing elevations of 7,000 feet to reach their final destinations. Not all of the salmon make it. Those that complete the journey must overcome many obstacles to spawn and bring forth a new generation of salmon.

How does the journey of the salmon relate to us? God said that tribulations, or great obstacles, would come against us because we live in a fallen world, *but also that we could overcome them.* (See John 16:33.) The fact is that God sees all of His children as world overcomers, but a lot of born-again, Spirit-filled Christians view themselves differently than God sees them. They see themselves in ways that are drastically— and tragically—different from the way God sees them. They perceive in themselves many faults, insecurities, and shortcomings. They consider themselves failures, incapable of accomplishing anything worthwhile. They feel defeated by bad habits, hardships, and financial troubles. Yet in the mind of God, their victory has already been established.

> *For whatsoever is born of God overcometh the world: and this is the victory that overcometh the world, even our faith.*
>
> (1 John 5:4)

No matter what adversity comes against you, God knows you can overcome it.

No matter what adversity comes against you, God knows you can overcome it. He knows because it has already been overcome. He is our ultimate victory over everything, most importantly, death, because He died for our sins and was raised from the dead.

Of course, it is one thing to know that God wants you to be an overcomer, but it is another thing altogether to experience this victory in your everyday life. To be a world overcomer, achieve everything that God has for you, and proclaim victory over whatever comes against you, you will have to surmount the inevitable obstacles that will try to keep you from fulfilling your destiny.

To accomplish this feat of overcoming, you will have to fight against currents that have been carrying you in the same direction for years and years. One of the strongest currents you will have to resist is an enemy that attacks all people, even Christians: fear.

Fear desires to overtake you, influence you to the point of control, and eventually weaken you so much that you're too enfeebled to go on. But you can live as an overcomer and achieve victory after victory. To do that, you first need to understand something.

Fear causes unnatural and discomforting emotions to develop within us. Unreasonable, tormenting, and persistent fear may destroy your peace and happiness. For some Christians, fear is so prevalent in their lives that they feel it is a part of their personalities, when the truth is that God did not design us to accommodate this type of fear. He certainly cannot give us what He does not possess Himself. Fear is not something you were born with; it is an emotion that is learned and can be developed to an excessive degree.

Again, the first biblical record of human fear appears in Genesis 3:10:

[Adam] *said, I heard thy voice in the garden, and I was **afraid**, because I was naked; and I hid myself.* (emphasis added)

A close examination of this encounter between God and Adam reveals that fear began with sin. Only after he sinned by defying God's orders and eating the forbidden fruit did Adam exhibit and express fear. (See Genesis 3:1–7.)

If you look closely at your own life and the decisions you have made, you can probably recognize fear as an underlying motive for many of these decisions. Perhaps fear and paranoia have become strongholds in your life. You may wonder how this could have happened.

According to the Bible, *"Faith comes by hearing, and hearing by the word of God"* (Romans 10:17 NKJV). Even though God's Word is the highest authority on earth, we often give more credence to the words of people than to God's Word.

In spite of the fact that God declares you to be an overcomer (1 John 5:4), your family, friends, and coworkers may not see you that way. This might account, in part, for your failure to see yourself this way.

WHOM ARE YOU LISTENING TO?

When looking at the formidable trek of the salmon, keep in mind that once the fish leaves the ocean and begins swimming upstream in freshwater rivers and streams, it encounters a lot of refuse and debris coming downstream against it.

In addition to evading all of the muck that gets in its way, the salmon has to be on the lookout for predators. Bears and large birds of prey eagerly feast on the salmon as it endeavors to reach its destination.

In the same way, when you set your course to overcome fear and follow your dream, you

When you set your course to overcome fear and follow your dream, you will have to navigate through fast-flowing, debris-filled currents.

will have to navigate through fast-flowing, debris-filled waters. In addition to dodging the garbage of self-doubt, insecurity, and timidity that is thrown your way, you must also be aware of predators that lie in wait.

Every day, you interact with a variety of people—family members, coworkers, friends, casual acquaintances, and complete strangers. Whether they are guiding you, counseling you, directing you, or offering you suggestions, you hear the words that are spoken—not only with your ears, but also with your heart and soul. Their words—whether good or bad, positive or negative, uplifting or degrading—can shape how you view yourself. They can have a significant impact on what you believe you can achieve and the goals you set out to accomplish.

If people constantly say the same things to you, over and over again, you will very likely begin to believe what they are saying. Wrong beliefs are often developed by constantly listening to—or hearing, heeding, and assimilating—words of rejection, condemnation, and degradation. Likewise, the right types of beliefs are developed by hearing—but hearing the Word of God, which is how faith comes. *"Faith cometh by hearing, and hearing by the word of God"* (Romans 10:17).

Negative words are to the psyche what radium and other radioactive materials are to the body. Some naturally occurring substances are classified as *radioactive*, meaning they emit radiation or have radioactive properties associated with them. The effects of exposure to radioactive materials are usually not immediate, but, over time, and depending on the amount of radiation to which people are exposed, the symptoms caused by prolonged exposure begin to manifest themselves.

Marie Curie, the Nobel Prize-winning physicist who isolated radioactive isotopes, discovered the elements radium and polonium and ultimately developed the theory she called "radioactivity." But while she was performing years of groundbreaking research, radiation exposure was taking its toll. She died of aplastic anemia, or leukemia, as a result, but this problem did not manifest for many years.

Something similar happens to people emotionally after prolonged exposure to negative words. But prolonged exposure to positive words— the truths and principles that fill the Bible—produces an effect, with opposite results: not death, but abundant life. We must expose ourselves continually to God's Word, which builds us up and strengthens our convictions about who we are in Christ. God's Word has properties that encourage and uphold us when we expose ourselves through hearing or reading the Word, as well as when we hear others preach and teach about it. We also benefit from studying the Scriptures and meditating (thinking, pondering) on them.

I encourage you to read the Word regularly. Search the Scriptures diligently, as they address and provide answers for the totality of mankind's needs. Believers should do this because the Bible is God's Word of instruction to those He has redeemed. According to the psalmist, it is *"a lamp unto* [our] *feet, and a light unto* [our] *path"* (Psalm 119:105).

Because the Word tells us who we are in Christ and instructs us how to live as faithful servants of God, we should give it a place of priority in our lives. So, whom are you listening to? Do the words of others have more authority in your life than the Word of God has?

If you are paying more attention to the negative, fear-inducing words people say to you instead of what Scripture says, you will eventually allow fear to dominate everything you do, including the things you say, the career opportunities you pursue, and any other goals you might try to accomplish.

Again, debilitating fear is not from God, and He does not want you to be dominated by it. This truth is quite clear in 2 Timothy 1:7, where Paul wrote that God did not give us a spirit of fear. Instead, He endued us with His power, His love, and sound minds, or the mind of Christ. (See 1 Corinthians 2:16.) God not only sees you as an overcomer, but He also sees you as fearless.

When God gives you an idea for a new business venture or when He wants you to minister words of comfort and healing to someone, He sees you only on the basis of His Word. He doesn't see you filled with fear, but rather filled with His abilities and wisdom. Now that you know this, you can no longer use the excuse, "But I'm timid and shy."

When you become a born-again Christian and are baptized in the Holy Spirit, you are filled with God's power and love. (If you have not yet been born again and filled with the Spirit, refer to the prayers and information in the back of this book to learn what is meant by *baptism in the Holy Spirit*.) God expects you to use the power He provides to overcome any fear that threatens to hold you back.

God knows the abilities that He has imparted to you. He knows that the same power that raised His Son Jesus[1] from the dead now dwells in you. (See Romans 8:11.) He expects you to use the strengths, talents, and perseverance with which He has equipped you.

CREATED TO RULE AND REIGN

At the beginning of time, when God created Adam and placed him in the garden of Eden, He told him, *"Have dominion over the fish of the sea, and over the fowl of the air, and over the cattle, and over all the earth, and over every creeping thing that creepeth upon the earth"* (Genesis 1:26).

God wants you to rule and reign on the earth, just as Adam did.

This command didn't begin and end with Adam. It was passed on to all of humanity, and it has not changed. God wants you to rule and reign on the earth, just as Adam did. Nowhere in the Bible does it say that we humans are to be at the bottom of the totem pole, holding up everything else.

No, God wants us to operate with dominion on this planet. God sees you as a ruler, one of His representatives endowed with stewardship rights over His creation. And this is how you must see yourself: as a ruler, and as one who overcomes any and every challenge that rises up against you.

Genesis 1:28 says, *"And God blessed them."* Another way to convey the meaning of the word *"blessed"* in this verse is with the phrase "empowered to prosper."[2] Think about that—God empowered man to succeed. He empowered us to be fruitful, to multiply, to subdue, and to have dominion. He did this at the beginning of time.

From God's perspective, the blessing that is upon you for success was instituted a long time ago and reinstituted through Christ. It is not something that you have to wait for God to do; it is already done.

Some people are waiting for God to bless them, not realizing that He already has. He is the one who's waiting—waiting for them to realize and walk in what is already theirs. God is out in front of us, saying, "Come on, walk with Me."

God Is My Friend

In the same way that God walked with Adam in the garden of Eden, He wants to walk with you. Before the fall, God did not walk ahead of Adam; the two walked side by side. They walked as friends, and that is how He wants to walk with you—as your friend.

As a youngster, I had a group of friends with whom I always hung around. We were buddies. When we walked home from school, we never walked single file. We were all on the same level, so we walked shoulder to shoulder; we talked face-to-face.

That is how God wants us to operate with Him. He is not some remote Supreme Being who is so far away that He is unreachable, untouchable, and unable to relate to us. On the contrary, He couldn't be closer—He dwells within us. (See John 14:20.) We were created so that He could dwell in us. Wherever we go, God goes with us. Whatever we face, we face with God. We never face anything alone.

We can be confident that whatever we face, we do not stand in our own strength but in the strength of God, because *"greater is he that is in you, than he that is in the world"* (1 John 4:4). God consistently encourages His people to be strong and of good courage for the simple reason that He is with us.

Seeing Yourself as God Sees You

To be the person God destined you to be, you must daily build His image of you inside yourself. I want to show you how to do that. It is imperative that you begin seeing yourself the way God sees you. Because you will *always* behave in a manner that is consistent with the way you see yourself, you will never rise above the level of your self-image. So if you see yourself as triumphant, you will experience victory.

On the other hand, if you see yourself as defeated, then, no matter how hard you try, something will *always* go wrong, sealing your defeat. If you believe that everything bad that could possibly happen will, in fact, come to pass, then nothing will ever go right for you. However, if you see yourself the same way God sees you, you will always feel ready to rise above any adversity that comes against you and to face down any fear that tries to bind you in passivity.

In the Bible, whenever God dispatched an angel to deliver a message to someone, such as Mary, Jesus' mother, or the shepherds, usually the first thing the angel said was "Fear not." This is important. The close proximity of a heavenly being—the very presence of God—was reason enough for these recipients not to give fear a place in their lives.

Can you imagine what your life would be like if you were not afraid of anything? Suppose you believed that you could never fail at anything. How would you behave? How would you live? How would you conduct yourself?

God sees you as a conqueror. He sees you as an overcomer, no matter what comes against you.

God sees you as a conqueror. He sees you as an overcomer, no matter what comes against you. In His mind, fear can never be justified. As far as He is concerned, there is no reason for you to be afraid about anything because He has given you everything you need that pertains to life and godliness. (See 2 Peter 1:3.) He has given you everything you need to be an overcomer.

CREATED IN GOD'S IMAGE

God said, *"Let us make man in our image, after our likeness"* (Genesis 1:26). Adam and Eve—humans—were the last beings God created, but He used no other creature as a model from which to form man. The design of mankind is entirely unique, different from every other type of living thing that God created.

Humans are unique because they are fashioned after God's image and likeness. This shows us that God unequivocally wants us to be as

He is. First John 4:17 says, *"As he [God] is, so are we in this world."* This is the perspective from which God sees us.

If God formed and fashioned us in His image and likeness, it follows that He wants us to be like Him. I would like to submit to you that God has a positive self-image. His self-esteem and self-respect are without question. Since we are created in His image, we, too, should have healthy, positive self-images.

In God's infinite wisdom, though we all resemble Him, each of us is a unique expression of Him and His nature. In other words, He will never run out of ways to express Himself in mankind, but, in spite of our diversity of skin tone, personalities, strengths, and other attributes, a common thread of divine character links us all together. We each have different talents and abilities, but our characters should be aligned with God and His Word.

Thinking the Way God Thinks

To live as an overcomer of this world, you must see yourself the way God sees you. If your self-image is a far cry from the image God paints in the Bible of His children, then you must change your perspective of yourself so that it matches what Scripture says about you. This shift in perspective is achieved by changing the way you think.

You must force yourself to think on *"whatsoever things are true, whatsoever things are honest, whatsoever things are just, whatsoever things are pure, whatsoever things are lovely, whatsoever things are of good report"* (Philippians 4:8). Thinking on what is true and good leaves no room in your mind for a stronghold of fear and negativity.

The Word declares that you are a conqueror, or an overcomer through Christ. (See Romans 8:37.) It also says that as you reflect God's character, whatever you do will prosper. (See Psalm 1:3.) *"God is not a man, that he should lie"* (Numbers 23:19), so if He said that you will succeed, then you will. Regardless of what a situation may look like, God's Word will triumph if you do not give up.

Remember that if you have been born again, you are a child of God, and He paid an inconceivable price—the blood of His only begotten

Son—for you to have fellowship with Him. Believe in His boundless love for you. In the same way that a loving parent would do anything to ensure his child's success, God made provision through His Word for your success in every area of your life.

Deuteronomy 28:1–2 says, *"And it shall come to pass, if thou shalt hearken diligently unto the voice of the LORD thy God,…all these blessings shall come on thee, and overtake thee."* To *"hearken diligently"* means "to hear with attention or interest, listen to…give heed…discern…perceive,"[3] or to listen "listeningly." In other words, you must give the Word of God your undivided attention and focus. Don't allow one word to fall by the wayside.

When you give your full attention to the Word and listen carefully to what God says about you, the Word of God will prevail, stamping out the fear that is trying to overtake you.

Only you can decide how you think. Your pastor cannot think for you, your parents cannot think for you, I cannot think for you—and neither can anyone else. If your self-image is so poor that you "think" you will never amount to anything, then this attitude will become a self-fulfilling prophecy. If you dwell on defeat, then that is how you will end up in life—defeated and forgotten, never having made the slightest impact on the lives of the people around you.

If, on the other hand, you choose to believe what the Word says about you and refuse to believe the unkind words other people have said to put you down, you can rise above their falsehoods, which contradict God's Word. Then, you can step out with fearlessness and go after your heart's God-given dreams and desires with unflinching determination.

SOWING THE SEED OF THE WORD

In the parable of the sower (see Luke 8; Mark 4; Matthew 13), Jesus compared the Word of God to seeds that have the potential to take root and bear fruit in believers' lives, depending upon how the believers receive them.

As the farmer was scattering his seed, some of it fell by the wayside—or along the path—and it was trampled upon. Other seed was devoured by birds. Some seed fell among the rocks, where it sprung up but quickly withered because it lacked moisture. And finally, some seed fell among the thorns; but as it grew, the thorns choked it out.

In school, students learn various principles of science, such as Newton's laws of motion, Einstein's theory of relativity, and other axioms that explain how and why things work. Laws of nature are described as an order, or relation, of phenomena that have no variation, regardless of changing conditions.

A spiritual law is one that is unalterable by any means, whether natural or artificial. It is a fact that has been established by God and supersedes any subclass of laws, natural or man-made.

One spiritual law is Galatians 6:7, which says, *"Be not deceived; God is not mocked: for whatsoever a man soweth, that shall he also reap."* It is a commonly known fact that if a seed is sown into the ground and cultivated properly with adequate sunshine and water, a harvest is forthcoming—it will germinate, sprout, and grow. Certain factors may interrupt the process, such as birds or insects consuming the seeds before they can germinate. Still other factors may affect the process—a drought may stifle growth and decrease yield, an invasion of weeds may choke out the seedlings. Yet these factors do not change the law that governs the growth process. What has been planted, if it is allowed to grow, will develop into a predetermined outcome. A sunflower seed will yield a sunflower; an apple seed will sprout into the beginnings of a fruit tree. The sowing of our words, thoughts, and deeds will inevitably yield a harvest in kind.

I am reminded of when my daughters planted marigold seeds in a flowerpot on the back porch of our home. They watered the seeds, fertilized the soil, and made sure they were placed in direct sunlight. In a few weeks, the seeds had sprouted, and the girls were excited. A few weeks later, they noticed another kind of plant in the flowerpot. My wife, Marjanita, explained that what they saw were dandelion weeds. Wind blows the seeds around, and because weed seeds are tough and hardy, they take root wherever they find soil. The girls were sad because they expected beautiful orange marigolds to grow up, not yellow dandelion weeds. Marjanita reminded the girls about the parable of the sower in Matthew 13:3–9.

> *And he spake many things unto them in parables, saying, Behold, a sower went forth to sow; and when he sowed, some seeds fell by the way side, and the fowls came and devoured them up: some fell upon stony places, where they had not much earth: and forthwith they sprung up, because they has no deepness of earth: and when the sun was up, they were scorched; and because they had no root, they withered away. And some fell among thorns; and the thorns sprung up, and choked them: but other fell into good ground, and brought forth fruit, some an hundredfold, some sixtyfold, some thirtyfold.* (Matthew 13:3–8)

Jesus explained in Luke 8:11 that the seed is actually the Word of God. However, in the first three places where the Word was sown, we see that the seed did not take root and was therefore unfruitful. From this, we are able to recognize that the factors that precluded the seeds' growth have parallels in the spiritual realm that affect the fruitfulness of God's Word in our own lives. We, too, often erect obstacles that would cause a crop failure of the Word in our lives, such as a lack of diligence in Bible study, neglecting to spend time in prayer to God, and quickly losing enthusiasm for our faith.

This parable sets forth three potential seed yields: thirtyfold, sixtyfold, and one-hundredfold. (See Matthew 13:8.) I believe this parable addresses a critical issue in human endeavor—the issue of completing the things that we set out to do, the things God wants us to do.

If we allow the first three soil conditions to prevail in our lives, we will accomplish nothing worthwhile, much less God-ordained.

The four soil conditions—hardened, stony, filled with thorns, and nutrient-rich—illustrate four possible conditions of the human heart, or spirit. All soil conditions but the last produced no yield or harvest whatsoever. It is my observation and belief that if we allow the first three soil conditions to prevail in our lives, we will accomplish nothing worthwhile, much less God-ordained.

The fourth condition, the good soil, provides an environment in which productivity can occur. Jesus said that the decision rests with us as to the degree to which we will produce a harvest. Our aptitudes for success depend on the qualities of our "soils," or the extent to which we are nourished by the Word of God and open and obedient to the leading of His Spirit.

God does not put a limit on faith, and neither does faith put a limit on God. Jesus said in Luke 8:15 that those with an *"honest and good heart"* hear and keep the Word, and that's when it becomes fruitful.

A choice has been set before you. Are you going to believe what God says about you, or are you going allow the opinions of other people to determine what you think of yourself?

Realize that if you continue believing the words of others that have shackled your life, you will remain as you always have been. With God, on the other hand, you will find that nothing is impossible for you to accomplish. That's certainly good news to me. What do you think?

Chapter 2

Removing the Fear Factors

For six years, the reality television show *Fear Factor* dared contestants to conquer common fears—gross foods, grotesque insects, heights, and so forth—by competing against one another in different stunts that challenged them physically, mentally, and even gastronomically.

In some episodes, after the contestants learned the nature of their challenge, a few of them quit on the spot. Crippled by intimidation, they immediately gave in to a presupposition that it would be impossible for them to accomplish that particular feat. So, they refused to even attempt it.

All of us have "fear factors" that try to dominate us. Like the television show contestants, some people are able to conquer their fears easily; for others, it is a long and harrowing process, if they undertake it at all. One thing is certain: how you handle your fears ultimately determines your success in life. The key to handling fear is drawing on the powerful properties found in God's kingdom principles.

A principle of the kingdom of God can be referred to as a *spiritual law*. Essentially, whatever God declares as absolute constitutes a kingdom principle. God, the sovereign King, has established principles by which His kingdom functions and by which His subjects must live and interact with Him.

Human beings are the inhabitants of a physical realm—the earth. We Christian believers inhabit yet another sphere—one that transcends time, place, and all other geographical distinctions. We belong to the church, a universal citizenship of believers. Thus, we are citizens of God's kingdom; we are His subjects. It could be said that Christians hold a duality of citizenship.

As citizens of God's kingdom, then, we are called to invoke and engage the principles of the kingdom of God in the sphere of our physical existence: the earth and its political and geographical areas. For instance, divine healing power may be appropriated by faith and prayer to effect recoveries and cures for human ailments and diseases. Biblical revelation and godly wisdom may be sought to discover and resolve human dilemmas and other difficult situations. Yet, so often, we give heed to fear and allow it to hinder the flow of God's power, which could otherwise resolve our difficulties.

THE FEAR OF THE LORD

Before we continue our discussion about fear, it is necessary that I take a moment to explain the type of fear that, as Christians, we are *supposed* to have: the fear of the Lord. The Bible distinguishes between the *"fear of the Lord"* (see, for example, Job 28:28; Psalm 111:10; Proverbs 1:7; Isaiah 33:6) and "plain old fear" (i.e., of spiders, heights, speaking in public, death, and so forth). The fear of the Lord consists of the reverence and respect that we reflect in a proper attitude and obedient behavior toward God. We are aware—and in awe—of His presence and power, which inspire us to govern ourselves accordingly, not taking our faith lightly or treating almighty God like a casual buddy. Scripture identifies a number of traits associated with the fear of the Lord, and they are beneficial to the well-being of our spirits, souls, and bodies.

The fear of the Lord consists of the reverence and respect that we reflect in a proper attitude and obedient behavior toward God.

The fear of the Lord:

• is clean and enduring (Psalm 19:9).

- lays up the goodness of the Lord on our behalf (Psalm 31:19).
- enables us to receive God's boundless mercy (Psalm 103:11).
- evokes His compassion (Psalm 103:13).
- is the beginning of knowledge (Proverbs 1:7).
- hates evil (Proverbs 8:13).
- is the beginning of wisdom (Proverbs 9:10).
- prolongs life (Proverbs 10:27).
- fosters strong confidence (Proverbs 14:26).
- gives us a place of refuge (Proverbs 14:26).
- is a foundation of life and protection from death (Proverbs 14:27).
- is better than great treasure (Proverbs 15:16).
- is the instruction of wisdom (Proverbs 15:33).
- strengthens our discernment so that we may depart from evil (Proverbs 16:6).
- brings satisfaction and spares us from evil (Proverbs 19:23).
- provides riches, honor, and a rewarding life (Proverbs 22:4).

We can develop the fear of the Lord by praying regularly, reading and studying the Bible, being obedient to God's Word, and following the guidance of the Holy Spirit.

Study to show thyself approved unto God, a workman that needeth not to be ashamed, rightly dividing the word of truth.
(2 Timothy 2:15)

This book of the law shall not depart out of thy mouth; but thou shalt meditate therein day and night, that thou mayest observe to do according to all that is written therein: for then thou shalt make thy way prosperous, and then thou shalt have good success.
(Joshua 1:8)

But be ye doers of the word, and not hearers only, deceiving your own selves.
(James 1:22)

For as many as are led by the [Holy] *Spirit of God, they are the sons of God.* (Romans 8:14)

TWO MAJOR FEARS

Now that you understand the "good" type of fear, let's return to our discussion of debilitating fears—those that keep us from proclaiming and procuring God's promises for our success. Long is the list of fears that control people. There are, however, two major fears that are primarily responsible for limiting the productivity, creativity, and ingenuity in all of us. The first of these fears is the fear of failure and loss. Ironically, this fear of failure is responsible for most failures in adults' lives. People are afraid to invest, afraid to risk, afraid to go forward, and afraid to take initiative. They are afraid to begin anything new because they fear it will fail, so they don't even try, thereby assuring the failure of the venture. Because they fear losing something, they hold to it tightly and never attempt anything. As a result, they never discover their potentials because they are clinging desperately to the little that they do have.

The second of these fears is the fear of criticism and rejection. This fear causes a lack of productivity among people who are so concerned about what others will say if they fail that they hold back and do nothing. They never venture beyond their comfort zones, for there, they feel safe and secure from damaging comments and disparaging words.

Constructive criticism from parents, teachers, pastors, and friends can help a young person to grow and mature.

These fears are learned early in life, often due to constant criticism. Not all criticism is negative, however. Constructive criticism from parents, teachers, pastors, and friends can help a young person to grow and mature. But destructive criticism, which is intended to cut down, not edify, is the catalyst of many fears. Let us explore in greater detail the divergent effects of destructive and constructive criticism on an individual.

An Illustration of Destructive Criticism

In this scenario, we will imagine that you are an avid gardener who takes great pride in the appearance of your yard. You have spent a great deal of time, effort, and money cultivating the yard and flower beds around your home.

One day, you are pulling your car into the driveway after work when you notice that all the petunias in your favorite flower patch have been broken and torn to shreds.

You park your car, then get out to inspect your prized plants. Noticing the bicycle tracks running through the flower garden—tracks that match the tread of your son's new bicycle—you realize that your very own son has destroyed your favorite garden plot!

At that precise moment, the young culprit whizzes by on his bicycle, nearly knocking you to the ground. You are so enraged that you begin screaming, "You stupid, clumsy kid! Don't you have sense enough not to ride that bike through my garden and tear up all my flowers? Thanks to your carelessness, my petunias are ruined! What's the matter with you? Do you have grits for brains?"

• • • • •

Remember, faith comes by hearing, and your child is likely taking in and assimilating into his psyche every word you just said about him. He is forming an opinion of himself based on your words, even if those words were more the products of a hot temper than a sincere opinion. If he hears only destructive criticism such as this, then the negative words you use will shape his self-image such that he will, in turn, criticize himself and believe that he is "stupid" and "clumsy," as you have said.

The next time he makes a mistake, he will repeat back to himself the words you have been saying over and over to him. "I have grits for brains. I am nothing but a stupid, clumsy kid."

An Illustration of Constructive Criticism

Let me show you how this same scenario could have been handled so that it yields a different outcome, this time with *constructive* criticism.

One day, you are pulling your car into the driveway after work when you notice that the petunias in your favorite flower patch have all been broken and torn to shreds.

You park your car, then get out to inspect your prized plants. Noticing the bicycle tracks running through the flower garden—tracks that match the tread of your son's new bicycle—you realize that your very own son has destroyed your favorite garden plot!

At that precise moment, the young culprit whizzes by on his bicycle, nearly knocking you to the ground. He skids to a halt. Taking a deep breath to calm your riled temper, you proceed to say, "Son, take a look at this. Do you see these ruined flowers? It looks as though you rode your bike through the flower bed, judging by the tire tracks. Did you do this? And is this what you meant to do?"

"No, Dad. I know how hard you worked to grow those flowers. I was just trying to keep up with the dog, but I accidentally steered off the driveway and through the flower bed."

"Okay," you say, "you didn't intend to ruin these flowers, but it happened. What do you suppose can be done to correct this?"

"I could help you to replant them, and I could be more careful when riding my bike."

An important component of constructive criticism is affirming the person's skills and worth. You conclude the discussion by saying, "I am glad that you learned to ride your bicycle so quickly. But let's work on improving control and being careful, okay?"

• • • • •

By talking with your son to reach a solution to the problem and to prevent future incidents of a similar nature, you teach him that he is not entrapped or defined by his mistakes. He does not have to be ashamed of what he did; rather, he will be inspired to try harder to avoid making the same mistake again. Most important, you will have corrected him without breaking his spirit.

If you are a parent, you must be responsible for training and teaching your children by both precept and example. Explain the situation to the errant child and guide him through the process of correcting it. Do not assume that he will know what to do. Work with him to analyze the problem, brainstorm possible solutions, and then choose the best one.

When your children misstep—and they will, just as you do—you want them to recognize that what they did was wrong, and why. But you do not want them to grow up thinking that they themselves are wrong. Once you fill a child with the belief that he or she is the problem, you have essentially destroyed his or her self-image.

If you are a parent, you must be responsible for training and teaching your children by both precept and example.

Children who believe that they are inherently wrong will start to think that they are incapable of doing anything right. Before long, their self-images—the images that you, as parents, teachers, or elders, have instilled in them by your negative words and harsh criticisms—will begin a cycle of perpetual failure in their lives.

THE TRUTH CAN HELP YOU GROW

Some people have received only destructive criticism throughout their lives. As a result, they are unable to distinguish between constructive and destructive criticism. To them, all criticism is destructive, intended to belittle and diminish. When some well-meaning person offers them advice, they tend to reject it automatically.

Instead of recognizing that *some* criticism may benefit them, they have programmed themselves to dismiss *all* criticism in order to protect their senses of self-esteem. They do not realize that constructive criticism can correct their situations, put them on better paths, help them to identify and correct bad habits, and improve the qualities of their lives. Instead, any criticism, destructive and constructive alike, is received as rejection.

At one time or another, everyone receives criticism. Sometimes, this criticism is constructive; other times, it's destructive. While you should never allow anyone to heap destructive criticism on you, you should not reject constructive criticism; if you do, you ignore advice that could help you to grow and succeed. Whatever it is that you constantly submit to—whomever you constantly heed—will have a significant degree of influence in your life. Conversely, whatever you resist will not be able to keep a grip on you.

If you constantly reject corrections made by people who are genuinely trying to help you, the influence of their constructive criticism will be weak and will prompt little to no positive change in your life. Instead of growing and maturing, you will remain in a lifestyle characterized by a pattern of failure, disappointment, hurt, and pain. You will not listen to anybody who tells you the truth about yourself, even when that truth has the potential to help you grow.

If you have constantly received destructive criticism, your self-image is probably rather poor. People who develop poor self-images have the capability of doing great things, but they are typically bound to mediocrity because they believe that they can do no better.

The effect of destructive criticism often manifests itself in a pattern of chronic failure. It causes a person to be timid and too afraid to become involved in anything. This is why some people settle into a comfort zone and keep doing the same things over and over again without taking a chance on something new or different. They do not want to do anything more or anything less. They refuse to be challenged or pushed.

God will challenge you to do things you have never done and prompt you to pursue feats that you never thought you could accomplish.

Know that God will push you. He will challenge you to do things you have never done and prompt you to pursue feats that you never thought you could accomplish. Then, after you have stepped out in faith to do as He has asked, He will challenge you to do even more.

Step Out in Trust

In his first inaugural address in 1933, during the height of the Great Depression, President Franklin D. Roosevelt spoke words of hope to a nation paralyzed with despair and despondent fear. He boldly declared, "The only thing we have to fear is fear itself—nameless, unreasoning, unjustified terror which paralyzes needed efforts to convert retreat into advance."

President Roosevelt understood the destructive potential of fear on a national level, but he also realized the need to deal with fear at the individual level.

Time after time, I have seen people held back and immobilized by fear and poor self-images. I always try to encourage such people to step out boldly and put their gifts and talents to use. For example, when I recognize certain traits or qualities in someone, I will usually ask him or her to help out in a particular ministry of the church where his or her gifts would be valuable. But I often get the answer, "Well, I don't know. To be honest with you, I really don't have the time."

Usually, time and availability have little to do with it. The truth behind this paltry excuse is that the individuals have poor self-images and are afraid of failure. So, instead of stepping into a position in which they will be challenged to grow, they come up with excuses as to why they cannot get involved. I have learned that people will say anything to avoid experiences that threaten to expose their fears and weaknesses, even if these same experiences might highlight their admirable traits, too.

The real issue is often that they are afraid to take charge of a situation and to tell other people what to do. Some people shy away from leadership roles because they fear rejection. With leadership often comes the responsibility to correct and evaluate those under you, and those who fear leading often worry that someone whom they correct will cease to like them. Rather than accepting the risk and taking the lead, they come up with excuses for why they cannot take on leadership responsibilities, and they merely continue to blend in with the rest of the congregation.

Some people shy away from leadership roles because they fear rejection.

They put on a good front, but they are only masking the real issue: fear. They have based their senses of self-worth on the opinions of other people, so if someone has a low opinion of them, then their own opinions of themselves drop to this same, reduced level.

This fear also explains why many people find that they are not promotable at work. Promotion is usually contingent upon the displayed abilities of leadership, assertiveness, and initiative. Those who seek promotion must have a desire and a drive to be, to become, to beget, to possess, and to belong, which is a basic urge of humanity.

I remember Roger. He was faithful in church attendance, but his willingness to volunteer in the church was hardly commensurate. When I asked Roger why he didn't want to volunteer to assist others, he listed one excuse after another. From his response, it was evident that he was trying to conceal a fear of something. After I inquired further, Roger finally admitted that he didn't volunteer because he felt he didn't meet the guidelines and requirements for volunteers in our ministry. He recognized that there was great blessing in volunteering, both to oneself and to others; however, the fear of failure was holding him back.

Roger admitted that his fears were based on the examples of other volunteers who had not fulfilled their commitments in service to God. Not wanting to "let God down" or to disappoint any of his fellow parishioners, Roger decided it was best just not to volunteer. Many times, examples such as Roger gave are the result of a failure to manage personal schedules, order priorities properly, and practice self-discipline.

Our volunteer coordinator presented Roger with the scriptural reasons why parishioners should support the ministry through volunteerism, based on 1 Corinthians 12:28–31:

> *And God hath set some in the church, first apostles, secondarily prophets, thirdly teachers, after that miracles, then gifts of healings, helps, governments, diversities of tongues. Are all apostles? are all prophets? are all teachers? are all workers of miracles? Have all the gifts of healing? do all speak with tongues? do all interpret? But covet earnestly the best gifts.*

God does not call everyone to preach or teach, but we all are called to assist, to lend a helping hand. Note the series of questions Paul posed in the passage above. They suggest that not all persons are called to use the gift of oracle ministry. Yet, in reference to the service of helps, there is no question. God has a place of "spiritual employment" for all of His people, whether in a leadership capacity or a supporting role.

With a newfound understanding of the scriptural mandate to offer help, and with further encouragement, Roger awakened to the church's need of his efforts, overcame his fear, and began volunteering regularly.

The enemy, Satan, will use other people to cloud your mind and confuse you about who you are in Christ. When you care excessively about others' opinions and become more concerned about which side of town you grew up on, what school you attended, and whom you call your friends than what God says about you, you limit what you can do on this earth and how you can influence the people around you.

The opinions of others are fickle, their praise fleeting, their standards always in flux. You might be popular one minute and a reject the next, just because of a silly rumor, an unstylish outfit, or an "uncool" activity. Conflicting messages come from all around: praises from your peers, punishment from your parents; acceptance by a church youth group, rejection by the popular group at school; commendations from your boss, bitter backstabbing from your coworkers. If the way you look at yourself depends on all these other views, you will become very confused, for the opinions of others are always changing.

God's estimation of you, on the other hand, is changeless. He loves you—He always has and always will. His opinion of you does not depend on your looks, talents, fame, or fortune, as others' do. No, He sees you as His precious child and a powerful overcomer, not because of who you are or what you do, but because His Son, Jesus Christ, died for your sins and rose again and now lives in you. You are beloved in His sight. Why not believe what God says about you instead of being influenced by what others say? Why not see yourself the way God sees you? If He sees you as fearless (and He does), then, with His help, you can start acting that way and overcoming your fears.

Why not believe what God says about you instead of being influenced by what others say?

Earlier, I asked you to think about what you would do if you were not afraid of anything. Let's revisit that question. How would you live if you knew you could not fail? How would your life be different if you walked fearlessly on the earth? What would you start doing right now that you have been too afraid to do? Where would you go and what would you say if you were no longer afraid?

I encourage you to step out and go to the places where you have been afraid to go, say the things that you have been afraid to say, and do the things that you have been afraid to do. Once you start acting as though you believe what God says about you, you may be surprised by how effectively it will prompt you to take fearless action.

FACE YOUR FEARS HEAD-ON

Early in her career, my wife worked for a major communications company. This job required her to travel to several states in the southeast region of the country. My wife loved her job, with one exception—these trips required her to travel on commercial airlines. Her issue with this requirement was a severe fear of flying. As someone who loves flying, I tried to convince her that there was no reason to be concerned and that the risks associated with flying were quite small when compared to a daily commute on the expressways around Atlanta. Although she appreciated my attempts to assuage her fears, it was only when she decided to confront her own fear head-on by courageously boarding that first business flight that she managed to conquer it. Looking to God and His Word, and boldly declaring her freedom from fear, she resolved to act courageously. She has been flying fearlessly ever since.

Some people may feel, after taking inventory of perceived personal disadvantages, that they are powerless in the face of obstacles on the path to victory over life's challenges. However, if you are willing to confront the resistant forces within yourself with persistence and endure the period of crisis that commonly accompanies the battle against fear, you will indeed prevail.

The Lord Jesus Himself encouraged such an approach to life through the parable of the persistent widow (also called the parable of the unjust judge). The account is recorded in Luke 18:1–8:

> *Then He spoke a parable to them, that men always ought to pray and not lose heart, saying: "There was in a certain city a judge who did not fear God nor regard man. Now there was a widow in that city; and she came to him, saying, 'Get justice for me from my adversary.' And he would not for a while; but afterward he said within himself,*

'Though I do not fear God nor regard man, yet because this widow troubles me I will avenge her, lest by her continual coming she weary me.'" Then the Lord said, "Hear what the unjust judge said. And shall God not avenge His own elect who cry out day and night to Him, though He bears long with them? I tell you that He will avenge them speedily. Nevertheless, when the Son of Man comes, will He really find faith on the earth?" (NKJV)

The compelling part of this story is how it contrasts what appears to be a significant obstacle (the unjust judge) and the seemingly insignificant toiler (the widow). All personal details that might be considered leverage for her case are left unmentioned—her age, ethnic origin, and so forth. Yet, her brave insistence that her case be heard indicates that the widow was drawing upon an internal sense of self-worth and zest for life.

Meditation on stories like this one may build strength and hope in your heart. Never forget that as a child of God, you always have your heavenly Father on your side. That means nothing is impossible for you to accomplish that falls within His will. As you look to Him, He will guide you every step of the way. You have only to trust Him and step out.

> *Never forget that as a child of God, you always have your heavenly Father on your side.*

The improper management of fear has no doubt accounted for many casualties in the body of Christ. To tackle this issue, we must not ignore it or deal with it superficially. One of the obstacles to dealing effectively with fear is a reluctance to face up to it and handle it properly. Dealing with fear can be uncomfortable and difficult, but the relief and peace that come when fear has been defeated are well worth the discomfort. So, let's conclude this chapter by exploring how to handle elements of fear in a godly way.

EFFECTIVE STEPS TO BREAKING FREE FROM FEAR

1. Establish the Truth

What is the reality of the situation? You may be facing only a fear and not a fact. Find a promise from the Word of God or a spiritual truth that can be used to counteract the fear.

For example, a person being considered for a promotion may suddenly feel that he is not capable of performing well at the next level. But the Bible says, *"I can do all things through Christ who strengthens me"* (Philippians 4:13 NKJV). This truth will boost his confidence and increase his reliance on God rather than on himself.

It is important to put things in perspective. When I face a difficult situation, I remind myself of what I call the most important question in the Bible: *"Is any thing too hard for the LORD?"* (Genesis 18:14).

2. Turn Your Thoughts to God and His Word

God and His Word are one. Essentially, God and love are one, for *"God is love"* (1 John 4:8, 16). And *"there is no fear in love; but perfect love casteth out fear"* (1 John 4:18).

Realizing that God loves us immeasurably, and loving Him in return, should put to rest any fears that bring torment, insecurity, and a host of other issues. Isaiah 26:3 says, *"You will keep him in perfect peace, whose mind is stayed on You, because he trusts in You"* (NKJV).

3. Submit Yourself to God

James 4:7 says, *"Therefore submit to God. Resist the devil and he will flee from you"* (NKJV). Fear is an influential and potentially overbearing force in many lives. But faith persuades us that God and His Word are more potent than our fears. Fear persuades you that the circumstances are more powerful than God and His Word. Faith will motivate you to forget fear and to please God in all things. *"But without faith it is impossible to please Him, for he who comes to God must believe that He is, and that He is a rewarder of those who diligently seek Him"* (Hebrews 11:6 NKJV).

4. Confess Freedom from Fear with Your Mouth

Take a deep breath and boldly declare in an authoritative voice, "I am free from fear, because *'if the Son makes you free, you shall be free indeed'* (John 8:36 NKJV). *'For God has not given us a spirit of fear, but of power and of love and of a sound mind'* (2 Timothy 1:7 NKJV). I declare that I am fear-free, in Jesus' name!"

Speak these verses as often as you need to: *"Seeing then that we have a High Priest who has passed through the heavens, Jesus the Son of God, let us hold fast our confession"* (Hebrews 4:14 NKJV). *"And since we have the same spirit of faith, according to what is written, 'I believed and therefore I spoke,' we also believe and therefore speak"* (2 Corinthians 4:13 NKJV).

5. Resolve to Act Courageously

Joshua 1:9 says, *"Have I not commanded you? Be strong and of good courage; do not be afraid, nor be dismayed, for the LORD your God is with you wherever you go"* (NKJV). As we discussed, courage is not necessarily the absence of fear but the ability to move resolutely and confidently in the face of your fears. It could be argued reasonably that one of life's greatest regrets is the failure to act courageously in the face of fear.

Chapter 3

Defusing the Ticking Time Bomb

On the NBC reality television show *The Apprentice*, eighteen candidates spend fifteen weeks competing for a job in the Donald Trump organization. The candidates are divided into two teams that become quasi corporations for the duration of the show season.

Each week, a project manager is chosen to lead his or her team through tasks they are assigned to complete—tasks designed to give the leaders an opportunity to showcase their leadership skills. The members of the corporation that "loses" at a particular task must face off with Mr. Trump himself in the dreaded boardroom, where he not only grills them on their mistakes but also listens intently to how the candidates assess and critique one another's job performances.

Some individuals will place all of the blame on other candidates, while others will be open, honest, and blunt. During each episode, it is easy to see how the candidates view themselves and how each of them operates in a manner that is consistent with his or her self-image.

Before deciding whom to fire, Trump asks two key advisers to critique the losing team's performance. Quite often, his decision is based on an issue of character and not on the amount of "widgets" that were sold.

On one particular episode, a project manager was fired because he repeatedly chose for a team member an individual who always relied on deceptive practices and manipulative tactics. Trump did not want his organization to include someone who would retain an employee prone to habitual lying, cheating, and stealing.

This example is not unusual; few CEOs desire dishonest employees, especially as members of their management staff. Yet stories of fraud, embezzlement, and other underhanded business practices seem to frequent the news more and more. What would cause a person to sway toward dishonesty? "Greed," you might say; "insatiable avarice." This may prompt many people to use unethical methods, but fear of criticism and rejection are underlying motivators that can make a person dishonest in order to preserve his or her reputation. Dishonesty is used even when dollars aren't at stake, so we can figure that fear underlies most underhanded practices in business, as well as in every other realm of life. The good news is that you can be free of fear.

In a post-9/11 world, where security has been tightened at airports, train stations, government buildings, and other public places, any pieces of luggage or packages that have been left unattended are confiscated and inspected to ensure that they contain no bombs or explosive devices. Anytime a package is left unattended at an airport or in an office building, people immediately think that a bomb might be in the package. The police and the bomb squad are called in, and they often evacuate the building or airport terminal until the contents have been tested and safety has been assured.

The fear of criticism and rejection is rooted in low self-esteem, which is a self-destructive force that can sabotage all your efforts.

Debilitating fears can be compared to a ticking time bomb. The fear of criticism and rejection is rooted in low self-esteem, which is a self-destructive force that can sabotage all of your efforts. Jesus came so you *"might have life, and that* [you] *might have it more abundantly"* (John 10:10), and He came to deliver you from low self-esteem. How can you have a poor estimation of yourself when God esteems you so highly? You are a magnificent creation whom He designed and loves immeasurably.

The men and women who work on a bomb squad risk their lives every time they answer a call. They know that an explosive device might be in the package and that it could explode as they try to defuse it. Nevertheless, they are determined to do their jobs and dismantle the bomb. Like the bomb squad, Jesus wants to defuse the time bombs that are set to go off on the inside of you.

DISMANTLING UNFORGIVENESS

Whether you realize it or not, you may have been assembling a bomb within you, piece by piece. If, early in life, you picked up some rejection and criticism, these influences may have resulted in poor self-esteem. Then, you probably began to harbor a buildup of anger, bitterness, and resentment.

Perhaps other people have told you that you would never amount to anything. They said that you would never succeed at anything. Maybe your dreams have been dashed throughout your life and you have given up all hope that anything good will happen to you.

You must understand that anytime you permit an unforgiving spirit to fester within you, anger and bitterness will set in, posing a serious hazard to your well-being. *Unforgiveness* is the unwillingness or inability to forgive. This attitude almost always manifests itself in the wake of an offense. Left unresolved, unforgiveness resides in the human personality like a ticking time bomb. Eventually, something will happen to cause the bomb to go off.

An *offense* is defined as "something that outrages the moral or physical senses;...the state of being insulted or morally outraged."[1] Some offenses are nothing more than minor misunderstandings and unintended hurts. But often, a minor offense, if left unresolved, can grow into a bitter grudge that is difficult to resolve. Other offenses may be severe and long lasting.

At other times, offenses are the result of deliberate and downright malicious words or actions. Whatever the cause of personal offense, the Bible instructs us to handle these issues in a scripturally appropriate manner.

Unfortunately, offenses are very common and, according to Jesus, inevitable. *"Then said he unto the disciples, It is impossible but that offenses will come"* (Luke 17:1). People not only take offense at remarks and actions, but they also cause others to take offense, whether deliberately or inadvertently.

When people are offended, they often experience hurt feelings, anger, resentment, indignation, and even outrage. An offense can be caused by countless things—an inappropriate word, malicious slander, a simple gesture, a menacing facial expression. Let's take a look at two primary causes of offense: an unruly tongue and a refusal to forgive.

AN UNRULY TONGUE

A common cause of offense is the tongue, from which issue all manner of harmful words, harsh criticisms, gossip, slander, snide remarks, and caustic sarcasm. James 3:2 states, *"For in many things we offend all. If any man offend not in word, the same is a perfect man, and able also to bridle the whole body."*

There are two observations that we may make from considering this verse. First, the ability to control one's tongue has a great impact on one's physical well-being—one who bridles his tongue is *"able to bridle the whole body."* Second, mastering one's tongue to the point of offending no one is an unlikely feat to achieve.

Knowing how harmful words can be, we should strive to use our tongues as benevolently as possible—not for cutting down, but for building up.

James pointed out that the person who does not offend in word is, in fact, a perfect man. In this context, the word *perfect* indicates complete maturity. We have all spoken words that have offended others, whether close friends, family members, or complete strangers. Likewise, we have been offended by similar words. Knowing how harmful words can be, we should strive to use our tongues as benevolently as possible—not for cutting down, but for building up.

James went on to say about the use of the tongue, *"But the tongue can no man tame; it is an unruly evil, full of deadly poison. Therewith bless we God, even the Father; and therewith curse we men, which are made after the similitude of God"* (James 3:8–9).

The powerful effects of the tongue also are outlined in Proverbs 18:21: *"Death and life are in the power of the tongue: and they that love it shall eat the fruit thereof."*

A REFUSAL TO FORGIVE

Another common cause of offense is unforgiveness. Holding grudges, nursing and rehearsing grievances, and "keeping tabs" on wrongful words, gestures, and deeds can certainly perpetuate an offense.

Unforgiveness is one of the negative traits considered antithetical to the nature of God. Life is simply too short to live in unforgiveness.

Some people are quickly offended for the slightest of reasons. Some offenses are obvious and deliberate, and people become offended for reasons that seem justifiable to any feeling person. All too often, however, offenses are not well-founded—we are ruffled by a sarcastic comment or an off-color joke and refuse to let it go.

Being sensitive can serve good purposes, but we should avoid being so sensitive that we become overly suspicious, critical, and cynical.

LETTING GO OF THE WIRES

When you accept Jesus as your Savior, He comes into your heart and begins the task of defusing the "bomb" of bitterness inside of you. He knows that any little spark has the capability to ignite the bomb and that the smallest of sparks can cause you to self-destruct.

In the natural, when a bomb squad begins to defuse a bomb, it follows a precise procedure. A series of colored wires must be cut in a particular order. If one wire is cut out of sequence, the bomb may detonate. When it comes to dismantling the ticking bomb of fears within you, the procedure differs in that you have to tell Jesus which wire you are willing to have Him cut first. It is up to you, not Him. And the color coding of your wires is unique. Perhaps the wires coated in red signify hurt. The blue wires may have abuse written all over them. The green ones might be wires of rejection.

The Master Bomb Defuser is waiting for you to "let go" of a wire. He cannot cut the hurt and bitterness of your past until you give Him the go-ahead to do so.

Some people try to keep certain wires hidden from Jesus because they are afraid of what He will think of them, just as they have been afraid of what other people would say if they knew about those wires. They may have a wire that is coated with abuse that they have kept hidden from everybody, so they try to keep it hidden from Jesus, too, forgetting that He already knows everything about them. (See Jeremiah 1:5; Psalm 139:1–4, 13–18.) They don't understand the love that He has for them—a love that is unconditional and independent of His omniscient knowledge of their sins, scars, and fears.

They think that when He "discovers" the truth about them, He will think less of them—that His opinion of them will change, and for the worse. They think that He is just like all of the people who have misunderstood their issues and judged them, inflicting great emotional anguish.

Without realizing it, they begin to hold on to their hurts, almost protectively. They seal themselves in pain, disappointment, humiliation, and shame. They endeavor to protect themselves and their reputations with silence and secrecy, but in doing this, they necessarily keep close by them the same issues that hurt them in the first place.

They believe that they can manage the pain and hurt on their own. They try to live with the humiliation, confident that someday, they will be just fine and everything will be okay.

That day never comes, however, and they remain exactly the same, day after day, year after year. Their harmful experiences, relived rather than released, retain great anguish, frustration, pain, hurt, and bitterness in their lives.

Even though what was done to them was terribly wrong, these types of feelings are never justifiable. People who have been hurt and become outraged at what has happened to them tend to assume that harboring bitterness is justifiable, even expected. But it is not justifiable.

By justifying the feelings of anger and indignation they have because of what was said or done to wrong them, they are actually holding on to the very thing that hurt them in the first place. They have been sinned against, but they cannot afford to allow bitterness to take root in their lives and sprout ineradicable weeds.

Scripture tells us, *"If we confess our sins, he is faithful and just to forgive us our sins, and to cleanse us from all unrighteousness"* (1 John 1:9). If we will only confess to Jesus what happened, acknowledging it and turning it over to Him, He will cut that wire and cleanse us from all wrongs, both experienced and committed.

THE PRINCIPLE OF RELEASE

Jesus, the Son of God, is able to defuse and remove all of the explosive emotional mechanisms you have picked up throughout your life. No matter what they are or how deeply embedded and intricately wired they may be, He has the ability to defuse them. And He not only defuses them but also replaces them with productive, fruitful mechanisms. You may wonder how this can happen.

Jesus, the Son of God, is able to defuse and remove all of the explosive emotional mechanisms you have picked up throughout your life.

The apostle John described what is known as the Principle of Release: *"Whosesoever sins ye remit, they are remitted unto them; and whosesoever sins ye retain, they are retained"* (John 20:23).

This verse tells us that whenever we hold grudges or harbor animosity against another person, we are actually holding on to that person's sins that he or she committed against us. In essence, we are binding whatever that individual did to us, and any emotional scars that resulted will grow only deeper.

Mitch made a verbal short-term loan of a few hundred dollars to Carl. Carl promised Mitch that he would repay the loan in full at the end of six weeks. At the conclusion of the six-week period, Mitch had not seen or heard from Carl. He tried several times to contact Carl, but Carl didn't respond. The more Mitch thought about his disappointment due to Carl's neglect, the more aggravated and disturbed he became. Mitch judged Carl as a debtor and a person who couldn't be trusted, even though they had been friends for more than ten years.

Mitch became miserable. His obsession with the outstanding loan was starting to dampen his usually cheerful personality. Finally, he prayed to the Lord about the matter. The Lord's response was, "Why don't you simply forgive Carl and release him from the debt?" This was not exactly the response that Mitch was expecting. He had envisioned the Lord dealing with the delinquent borrower, forcing him to repent and pay, in full, the debt he owed.

Considering the Lord's counsel, Mitch made the decision to forgive Carl and release him from the debt. He later testified that the moment he had fully resolved to do so, he was released from the bondage of anger and bitterness he was holding against Carl.

Interestingly, the very issues we hold against others have a way of penetrating our own lives. Why is this? Again, Jesus said in John 20:23, *"If you forgive the sins of any, they are forgiven them; if you retain the sins of any, they are retained"* (NKJV). Remember that all sin is ultimately against God, not against us. The effects of Mitch's constant focus on the wrong Carl committed against him actually began to work against him rather than mitigating the problem. Thus, Mitch did well to follow the exhortation found in 1 Peter 5:6–7: *"Therefore humble yourselves under the mighty hand of God, that He may exalt you in due time, casting all your care upon Him, for He cares for you"* (NKJV).

It should be noted that Mitch's response to the Lord in no way condoned Carl's negligence. He simply surrendered Carl's offense—and his own offended spirit—to the Lord, who then preserved Mitch's spiritual well-being. By the way, shortly after his decision to release Carl, Mitch received a sum of money well in excess of the delinquent loan from a source altogether different and unexpected!

I wonder how many times similarly petty offenses occur in the lives of other people and prompt disproportionate reactions of indignation. Offenses come in as many different packages as there are people. Maybe you've heard, or even said, something like the following: "The Pastor didn't call," "The usher didn't seat me in my favorite seat," "The greeter didn't shake my hand," "They looked the other way when they saw me coming," "When I picked up Tommy from the nursery, his diaper was wet."

Often, when someone has sinned against you, that person quickly forgets how he has hurt you. He may not even realize that what he said or did caused you pain. Oblivious, he moves on, leaves the situation behind, and goes about his business. Meanwhile, you dwell on his transgression and become mired in it, weighed down and unable to move forward.

Every time that person's name comes up, a signal goes off inside of you that triggers negative feelings and rage. Whenever you see that person, you go out of your way to avoid him or her. When this happens, the bomb mechanisms begin to move. The clock starts ticking.

God wants to stop the ticking time bomb and deliver you from your building anger. He wants you to live an abundant life while you are on the earth. (See John 10:10.) He does not want you to be bound by the past. But you must let go of your past and its painful traces.

God does not want you to be bound by the past. But you must let go of your past and its painful traces.

The key to being released from bondage to anger over what someone has done to you is to release that person—to forgive him or her, absolving the guilt. By doing this, you are not condoning what the individual did to you, nor are you allowing yourself to be a doormat to be walked upon. Rather, you are letting go of that transgression so that it no longer shackles you. Then, you can move forward in life.

THE BEST DEFENSE AGAINST OFFENSE

When you make the decision to reject and dismiss all of the negative things that have been said about you, you are releasing yourself from the hurt, anger, bitterness, and other harmful feelings that hold you captive.

Forgiving people for wrongful behavior and attitudes toward you does not come easily or automatically. It requires a decisive act of the will. While your mind comes up with reasons to justify the pursuit of revenge and paybacks, your spiritual well-being is contingent on your choosing instead to exercise the Principle of Release.

You may have been hurt by your parents, but do not hold them ransom at the price of your own emotional stability. You may have been hurt by your husband or wife, but do not hold your spouse hostage. Do not ascribe blame to anyone who has hurt you, however deeply, even if the fault was not your own. Instead, release the individual and get on with your life.

A Personal Example

Deliverance from an offense, as with other interpersonal conflicts, is not necessarily remedied by a formulaic application of what we consider to be an airtight working knowledge of the Word of God. God has an interesting way of informing us that He did not create a world in which He would not be needed. How thankful we should be, as believers, to be in a position to "see" the kingdom of God—that is to say, to perceive God at work in our own lives and in the lives of others around us.

Very early in my walk with the Lord, I heard news that a very popular and outstanding teacher of the Bible was scheduled to appear at a local church in our area. My wife, Marjanita, and I were very excited and made plans to attend.

When the day of the event arrived, we drove to the church in great anticipation. The parking lot was filling quickly with cars, and we had to park many yards from the building. We got out of the car and were walking toward the church when, to our surprise, we saw the guest speaker! He had just arrived, and he and a traveling companion were unloading materials from the trunk of his vehicle.

Excited for the opportunity to speak personally with him, I approached him and said loudly, "Hello! I really enjoy your ministry on the radio!" He turned and nodded, giving a slight smile. I thought he should have said more, maybe even started a conversation or something. Naturally, I felt slighted and thought that he should have appreciated my recognition of his greatness. But I would later realize that this was simply my spiritual immaturity and pride licking their wounds. What I should have done was offer to assist him in gathering his materials for his meeting, knowing that he was going to deliver a word from God and that he shouldn't have to be concerned with gathering materials. After all, I was there to hear him teach the Word of God!

As a result of the unpleasant encounter, I found it extremely difficult to focus during the teacher's presentation. In the car on the way home, I voiced my disappointment to my wife, and by the time we were home, I had essentially resolved in my mind not to listen to this Bible teacher ever again.

Soon after this episode, however, God saw to it that I was tuned in to a radio broadcast on which another Bible teacher was speaking about spiritual maturity. He described the stages of spiritual growth and maturity, contrasting the process with the stages of natural human development. I quickly identified myself in the childlike stage of spiritual development, and I began to repent to the Lord. I saw how foolish I had been to take offense at the Bible teacher's brief salutation. He was deflecting the glory to God, and I didn't realize it. I further understood that in doing so, he was exercising a high level of spiritual maturity by humbly accepting the praise I had given with silence akin to censure.

God may not always explain Himself, but He certainly does reveal Himself. Had I left it unresolved and unforgiven, this experience of offense could have robbed me of much spiritual wealth and wisdom. God graciously opened my eyes to understand the reality of the situation, and He helped me through what otherwise could have hindered my ability to receive wisdom from anyone ministering His Word. God gave me another encounter with the Bible teacher by whom I was offended, and by that time, I had a better understanding of spiritual growth and a knowledge that one of the enemy's tactics was to derail my God-given purpose through offense, bitterness, and strife. But the enemy did not prevail!

God may not always explain Himself, but He certainly does reveal Himself.

This experience was also vital in teaching me how to be led continually by the Holy Spirit. Yielding to the corrective instruction of the Lord ushered me further into the presence of one of the key mentors of my life and ministry.

Getting the Stains Out

When you release or remit another's offenses against you through the act of forgiveness, you prevent the effects of that sin from lingering in your own life. If you choose to retain the offense and ruminate on it, however, the toxic effects will become absorbed gradually, indiscernibly, into the fabric of your own character. And once the stain of an offense shows up, it is difficult to remove.

I like to use the example of laundering a shirt to illustrate this point. When I choose a white dress shirt from my wardrobe to wear with a suit, the shirt is clean, starched, and pressed. It is brilliantly white without spot or wrinkle.

Unfortunately, I am notorious for dripping food on my shirts when I am eating. Whenever this happens, the stain stands out against the once beautifully laundered garment and is very noticeable.

I may try to *cover* the stain by buttoning the front of my suit jacket, but that act does not *remove* the stain. Until I *choose* to launder the shirt, I will *retain* the stain, which has been *absorbed* by the fabric.

Various cleaning agents can be applied to *release* my shirt of its stain and restore it to its original, immaculate whiteness. This restoration does not happen, though, until I have *decided* to get the stain out.

The same is true for you when someone has stained your heart with harmful words or actions. Heard often enough, negative words and insults may become ingrained in the fabric of your psyche like indelible stains in the fabric of a shirt.

Too many people are looking outside—to the ones who have caused the hurt—to find relief. But blaming others and reveling in one's own innocence will neither help nor heal. These people should be looking on the inside, focusing on the words and experiences that they have permitted to paralyze them and hold them captive.

The problem is not on the outside of you but on the inside. Your hurt cannot be released as long as it is anchored in someone else and his or her wrongdoing. If you are clinging to bitterness and blame, your grip is too tight to release the problem. The issue is within you, and you must deal with yourself, asking God for help.

It is when you release the person who has hurt you that Jesus is able to cut a crucial wire in the ticking bomb. Once the wire has been cut, the bomb cannot go off; it is rendered powerless and will not explode.

Then, and only then, can healing touch your heart and set you free from the pain that has held you in bondage for so long.

Chapter 4

The Power of Imagination

As a young boy, I spent several summers working at my father's business in Philadelphia, Pennsylvania. Each day, I would walk about six blocks between our home and his business. This daily ritual was rather easy, especially during daylight hours. I would pass many row houses whose front steps were frequently occupied by neighbors enjoying the fresh air and warm sunshine. Over time, I got to know many of them by face, even stopping on occasion to engage in brief conversation.

My trek usually began in the morning or early afternoon, when I could clearly see everyone and everything along the way. These conditions established a feeling of safety in my mind. But at night, when I would make my way home, all that seemed to change. The blocks of row houses were lit dimly by the street lights situated at each street intersection and at the middle of each block. Although each city block might measure only about six hundred feet, the distance of my trek home through the dark always seemed like a mile or more.

If any people were outside at night, I could see their silhouettes, but few facial features, if any, were distinguishable. And the people who were out at night weren't always the same people I had observed during my morning walk.

The sounds of the city—cars, buses, people laughing and yelling—seemed amplified during the day. At night, the streets were more subdued, and at times, it grew eerily silent.

I experienced a distinctly different feeling when I took this journey at night. There was an uneasiness brought on by the darkness. I couldn't be absolutely certain about my surroundings; I couldn't tell the identity of each person I passed or encountered. Sometimes, I was startled by a voice or noise, its source obscured by the shadows.

At night, it seemed more common for a siren's scream to pierce the silence. Familiar though I was with the route of my walk and my whereabouts, I was always aware that something was missing—the feeling of assurance that I felt during the day, when sunlight illuminated everything and gave me a sense of security.

Day or night, I never felt safer than when I was on the front steps of my own house or, better yet, inside the door. I had a need to fill the dark and sometimes silent void with imaginary sights and sounds that I associated with security. I would pretend to drive a make-believe bus, stopping at corners to pick up and drop off my imaginary passengers. This activity helped to take my mind off the feelings of uneasiness—the feeling of fear that something I couldn't see might surprise me—and gave me a sense of security, however illusory.

Using my imagination to conjure positive and familiar pictures in my mind drove fear into remission. That remedy was temporary, at best. Thanks to God, I now know the truth of God's Word and walk in freedom from fear—day and night, in darkness and in light.

Fear is often learned in the classroom, right alongside reading, writing, and arithmetic. If you don't believe me, consider your own experiences as a young student. Think back to a time when your teacher posed a question to the class, then asked, "Who will be the first to answer?"

Probably no more than a few students raised their hands. Many, if not most, hands remained down. Why? Uncertainty. Fear of being wrong. Paranoia about being perceived by your peers and teacher as incompetent or stupid. An incorrect answer, especially when voiced in front of one's classmates (as opposed to an incorrect answer on an exam, which the teacher alone sees), is usually viewed as a type of failure. Many students are petrified of being corrected in front of their peers, and this fear of failure often extends into adulthood, where our peers are coworkers, neighbors, or fellow church members. They grow up either thinking *I'm a failure* or doing nothing to avoid being one.

It is important to realize that failure is not a person; failure is an event. You have probably experienced failure in your life, but that does not make you a failure. Take, for example, a businessperson who succeeds in attracting a new corporate client. This single successful business deal does not make the individual responsible a successful businessperson. What if it was his first success in three years of consecutive failed ventures? Likewise, a single business deal that falls through does not make that same individual an unsuccessful businessman. One instance of success does not propel you to the pinnacle of your profession; one instance of failure does not plunge you hopelessly into quicksand.

You have probably experienced failure in your life, but that does not make you a failure.

Whatever your career path or pursuit, as long as you get up one more time whenever you are knocked down, you will keep moving forward. Success, therefore, is really attained by refusing to quit.

Success requires resilience. It requires what I like to call "Holy Ghost bounce-back." Successful people are those who maintain positive, persistent attitudes in spite of any knockdowns and pitfalls they experience. Regardless of what happens to them, they persevere. They do not allow self-limiting beliefs to keep them from moving forward.

You will always behave in a manner that is consistent with the way in which you see yourself. As Proverbs 23:7 says, *"For as* [man] *thinketh in his heart, so is he."*

Your life will follow the direction of your most dominant thought pattern, or mind-set, so, you see, you will never rise above the level of your self-esteem. In other words, you can soar as high as your self-esteem will let you.

The word *esteem* is defined as both a noun and a transitive verb. In other words, it is something that also *does* something. As a noun, *esteem* means "the regard in which one is held."[1] As a transitive verb, *esteem* means "to view as: consider...to set a high value on: regard highly and prize accordingly."[2]

Self-esteem has to do with the personal evaluation or opinion of one's own worth, competence, and importance. Although it includes our thoughts, feelings, and attitudes toward ourselves, it might have nothing to do with reality—how you really are. Self-esteem can be negative or positive, and the type will determine the outcomes of a person's use of his or her gifts and talents.

Consider, for example, a talented pianist. If he has low self-esteem, he will censure himself harshly when he makes mistakes and eventually give up, thinking, *I could never be a great musician.* His self-defeating attitude will keep him from being a successful musician. A talented pianist with high self-esteem, on the other hand, will be confident in his abilities, proud of his skills, and accepting of feedback from his teacher. He will view challenging pieces as opportunities to improve and worthy challenges to surmount. Because he believes in himself, he will go on to become a successful musician.

Poor self-esteem can blind someone to his or her true potential, which results in many a tragic loss of potential. Overly inflated self-esteem can also blind people to reality. Take the contestants of the television talent show *American Idol*, for example. If you have seen the preliminary tryouts, in which would-be divas and hopeful entertainers strut their stuff, you have seen that many of them overestimate the scope and level of their talents. Granted, some know that they can't sing; they simply want to be on TV. Lucky for them, they care little, if at all, about what others think of them. But many contestants are crushed by disappointment or shocked in disbelief when they don't make the cut, even when it is obvious that they have no musical skill to speak of. It is important to have healthy, high self-esteem—not to be confused with egocentric conceit—which is built upon the confidence that comes from knowing that you are a child of God and experiencing the great love with which He created and saved you.

Feelings of inferiority and worthlessness plague people with poor self-esteem. This phenomenon is so common that it affects people from all walks of life—even born-again believers. This must not be.

It is important to embrace your identity in Christ, knowing that He loves you as someone uniquely gifted for serving in His kingdom.

PRODUCTS OF POOR SELF-ESTEEM

Poor self-esteem is a burden that oppresses, and it can be viewed as a spiritually cancerous condition that corrupts our thoughts, emotions, attitudes, values, and actions. A poor self-image sows the seeds of many destructive symptoms. Some of the products of poor self-esteem include:

It is important to embrace your identity in Christ, knowing that He loves you as someone uniquely gifted for serving in His kingdom.

- Harsh self-criticism
- Self-hatred
- Self-rejection
- A nagging feeling of being unwanted
- Feeling unneeded
- Diminished sense of self-worth and self-confidence
- Gradual withdrawal from other people; increased isolation
- Stifled initiative
- Quenched motivation
- Reinforced feelings of inadequacy, hopelessness, and weakness

Poor self-esteem often masquerades as other attitudes. It is sometimes camouflaged by a negative, complaining, and argumentative spirit. The effects include jealousy, an unforgiving attitude, resentment, intolerance, and suspicion toward others. Some other symptoms may include being overly sensitive, moody, depressed, and introverted. Ultimately, these issues all stem from fear.

Maybe you're suffering from low self-esteem and you wonder what—if anything—you can do to turn this around. Good news! God gave each of us an important piece of built-in equipment that we can use to develop or improve our levels of self-esteem. It is called *imagination*.

More Than Child's Play

I grew up in a row house in inner-city Philadelphia. My childhood friends and I would search for "treasures" in the garbage our neighbors set by the curb for waste management to pick up. To this group of young boys, "treasures" included such things as worn-out roller skates, planks of lumber, and trash can lids.

We made swords out of the lumber we found, and we "borrowed" the neighbors' trash can lids to use as shields. We imagined that we were Vikings or gladiators, and we fought endlessly to take control of our enemies' fortress. The "fortress" may have been nothing more than a mere street corner, but to us, it was a formidable bastion to conquer.

Long before any of us got a driver's license, we traveled without cars on a homemade vehicle of transportation. We cut a two-by-four in half and then split the wheels on a pair of roller skates. Then, we nailed the front wheels to the front of the two-by-four and the back wheels to the other end of the board. Next, we took a soda crate, which we had decorated with hundreds of bottle caps nailed to its exterior, and attached it to the two-by-four. When construction was complete, we were the proud owners of a homemade scooter.

We searched for enough wood, broken roller skates, and crates until we were able to make scooters for every boy and girl on the block. Together, we were the First Mechanized Division of Main Street.

We pretended we were drafted into the military and became the armored personnel of tanks and military vehicles. Each of us had a different rank and corresponding task to carry out. We planned maneuvers and fought battles. We even staged casualties. Some of the boys were "stabbed" and fell over, feigning death. Of course, anyone who "died" eventually came back to life—we needed their help to plan out another attack!

At other times, we would pretend that a front porch was a sailing ship and that the sidewalk just below was the ocean water. We were pirates of the Caribbean long before Walt Disney Pictures made the movie!

In reality, we were just a bunch of neighborhood kids finding ways to stay occupied and entertain ourselves. But when we were playing, we were army generals, seafaring scalawags, and fierce gladiators—and nobody could convince us otherwise. We used our imaginations to become people other than ourselves, heroes of another time and place.

Playing pretend and using one's imagination are applaudable activities, at least among children. Sadly, when imaginative children turn into adults, they often leave these "childish" pastimes in the playroom. Using one's imagination is an unspoken taboo for "mature" adults, an activity encouraged on the playground but outlawed in the boardroom. But God never intended for imagination, which includes faith, to be a faculty abandoned after childhood. He wants us to pray and then believe, or imagine, we have received our requests. (See Mark 11:24.) Youth gives us an opportunity to develop our imaginations, not exhaust them. God did not design our imaginations for mere child's play. He wants us to use our faith and imaginations into adulthood, as well.

God never intended for imagination, which includes faith, to be a faculty abandoned after childhood.

THE ROOT OF IMAGINATION

When Jesus was passed over again by ship unto the other side, much people gathered unto him: and he was nigh unto the sea. And, behold, there cometh one of the rulers of the synagogue, Jairus by name; and when he saw him, he fell at his feet, and besought him greatly, saying, My little daughter lieth at the point of death: I pray thee, come and lay thy hands on her, that she may be healed; and she shall live. And Jesus went with him; and much people followed him, and thronged him. (Mark 5:21–24)

These verses begin the account of Jairus, a ruler of the synagogue, whose young daughter was apparently terminally ill. On His way to minister to her, Jesus encountered the woman with the issue of blood.

Imagination played a big part in giving her the faith to touch the hem of Jesus' garment and receive His healing power in her body.

We'll talk more about her later on, but imagination played a big part in giving her the faith to touch the hem of Jesus' garment and receive His healing power in her body.

Life would be simple if we could address just one issue at a time, but that would not be an accurate picture of reality. Let's pick up the story after Jesus' encounter with the woman.

While he yet spake, there came from the ruler of the synagogue's house certain which said, Thy daughter is dead: why troublest thou the Master any further? (Mark 5:35)

Notice the lack of faith and imagination on the part of the "certain" ones from Jairus' household. They couldn't see how Jesus could possibly help that little girl now. Jesus immediately stopped their negative mind-set from spreading to Jairus.

*As soon as Jesus heard the word that was spoken, he saith unto the ruler of the synagogue, **Be not afraid, only believe.** And he suffered no man to follow him, save Peter, and James, and John the brother of James.* (Mark 5:36–37, emphasis added)

Herein lies the root of faith and imagination: *"only believe."* Notice, too, that Jesus took only a handful of men with him—those who shared His imaginative mind-set.

He cometh to the house of the ruler of the synagogue, and seeth the tumult, and them that wept and wailed greatly. And when he was come in, he saith unto them, Why make ye this ado, and weep? the damsel is not dead, but sleepeth. And they laughed him to scorn. (Mark 5:38–40)

The use of imagination affects people in all walks of life. From the boardroom to the battlefield to the bedside, the strength of one's imagination (or a lack thereof) yields a telling projection of the course of an individual's life. In the next part of this story, we see how Jesus handled these faithless, unimaginative people.

When he had put them all out, he taketh the father and the mother of the damsel, and them that were with him, and entereth in where the damsel was lying. And he took the damsel by the hand, and said unto her, Talitha cumi; which is, being interpreted, Damsel, I say unto thee, arise. And straightway the damsel arose, and walked; for she was of the age of twelve years. And they were aston-ished with a great astonishment. (Mark 5:40–42)

In this account, Jesus, upon arriving at the residence of Jairus, pushed aside potential hindrances to the flow of God's power. In this case, it was a group of mourners who ridiculed Jesus' assessment of the child's condition because they couldn't see or imagine anything beyond the physical circumstances. After He sent away those with no imagina-tion, Jesus proceeded to minister successfully to the child in the pres-ence of her parents and a few of His disciples.

The Bible clearly shows lack of imagination—unbelief—to be a significant hindrance to the power of God. (See Mark 6:5.)

DREAMING THE IMPOSSIBLE

In our ministry, my wife and I have had an experience similar to the story of Jairus and his daughter. We received a call from the fam-ily of an individual who had been diagnosed with a terminal illness. They wanted us to minister to her, so we immediately proceeded to the hospital. Upon arriving, we found several family members and friends of the patient gathered inside her room and in the hallway just outside. There was no talk of faith or healing in any conversation. They couldn't imagine such a possibility for this person and had simply accepted her imminent death as inevitable. My wife and I tactfully requested those gathered to vacate the room; as soon as they left, the entire atmosphere changed dramatically.

The patient, in her mid-sixties, had grown visibly embittered by the nature of her circumstances, and her friends and relatives had found little success in cheering her. In fact, she refused to talk or eat, but she was very aware of our presence, as we were strangers. The situation was rather awkward, but the Holy Spirit prompted me to ask her a question: "Do you want to be healed?"

One might deem this question ridiculous—who wouldn't want to be healed? However, the Lord reminded me of the man at the pool of Bethesda of whom He had asked the very same thing. (See John 5:2–11.) This woman rolled her eyes at me as if to say, "You ought to know that I want to be healed."

With some encouragement, she began to converse more freely. We assessed that she didn't have any real substantive knowledge about God's Word. (Later on, we'll talk more about the Word in relation to what we think, but know that it has everything to do with being able to imagine what seems to be impossible in the natural realm.) We decided to remedy that.

We taught her the basics about coming into a relationship with God through Jesus and told her about God's healing power. At this point, a noticeable change came across her countenance. We also noticed that her friends and relatives who had been gathered earlier had left the premises altogether. By the end of our visit, the woman had become cheerful and expressed confidence that she, too, would be healed by the power of God.

Later, we received another phone call from the same relative who had requested our visit. This person expressed amazement at the complete turnaround of the sick woman's attitude. A few days later, the doctors examined several X-rays they had taken and found that the malignant tumor had vanished. The woman was declared well and was released from the hospital. They expected her to live a long, full life.

Newly armed with the knowledge of God and His Word, this woman experienced a radically transformed belief system and was able to believe, or imagine, herself healed. The same can be true for you.

I once read a newspaper article about a man who had just passed away at the age of ninety. His name was Joseph J. Zimmermann Jr., and he was credited with inventing one of the first commercially successful telephone answering machines. Compared to the voice mailboxes we use today, his device was extremely large and crude.

Zimmermann's answering machine was equipped with a mechanical levered arm that would lift the receiver off the phone cradle when the telephone rang. Then, a 78-rpm record would play a prerecorded message, informing the caller that the person whom he or she was trying to reach was not available. When the message had finished playing, the caller had the option of leaving a message up to thirty seconds in length, which was recorded by a wire device.

Before his idea was realized, I am sure that some people called it a crazy notion. Imagine—a telephone answering itself, giving a greeting, and recording information that could be played back later by the intended message recipient. Who had ever heard of such a thing? Like other innovators, from Thomas Edison and electricity to the Wright brothers and airplane flight to Edward Jenner and the smallpox vaccine, Zimmermann probably had to ignore many naysayers in order to persevere in fulfilling the goal that started in his imaginative, inventive mind.

Let me encourage you to begin imagining the fulfillment of God's promises for your life. Create a positive self-image by imagining who the Bible says you are in Christ. Remember, you were created in the image and likeness of God. You are not worthless, or without value. Although you are highly esteemed by God, you can devalue your worth with a poor self-image.

Create a positive self-image by imagining who the Bible says you are in Christ.

Your self-image sets the course for your future. You will act according to how you see yourself. When your self-image is poor, you will have little hope for a promising future, and you will probably not even try to make a better way for yourself. But when you see yourself as God sees you, you will have hope for a bright future. Whatever you imagine and have faith for can come to pass. You can do all things through Christ, who strengthens you. (See Philippians 4:13.) *"Delight thyself... in the LORD; and he shall give thee the desires of thine heart. Commit thy way unto the LORD; trust also in him; and he shall bring it to pass"* (Psalm 37:4–5).

Chapter 5

Driving Out the "Ites"

After the death of Moses, Joshua was commissioned by God to lead the children of Israel across the Jordan River and into the Promised Land. (See Deuteronomy 34:5, 9; Joshua 1:1–9.) But there was a problem. This land of promise was full of "ites": Jebusites, Perizzites, Ammonites, Amorites, and Canaanites.

Contrary to what the Israelites would have preferred, when they crossed into the land of milk and honey, the "ites" did not leave automatically. Instead, they had to be driven out before the Hebrew children could possess the land that God had promised to them.

The "ites" represented internal issues that the children of Israel had to face and deal with before they could enter into and inhabit the Promised Land. These issues included fears and phobias they had accumulated during their years of enslavement in Egypt and throughout their forty years of wandering in the wilderness.

These fears limited the Israelites. For example, Numbers 13 tells how Moses sent twelve spies into the Promised Land to scope out the prospects. When the spies returned, only two of them—Joshua and Caleb—believed that they could conquer the "ites" and possess what God had promised.

The remaining ten spies disagreed, saying,

The people be strong that dwell in the land, and the cities are walled, and very great: and moreover we saw the children of Anak there....We be not able to go up against the people; for they are stronger than we....And there we saw the giants, the sons of Anak, which come of the giants: and we were in our own sight as grasshoppers, and so we were in their sight.

(Numbers 13:28, 31, 33)

Even though God had delivered them from the Egyptian army by parting the Red Sea for them to pass through, and even though He had miraculously provided for them in the wilderness, giving them manna and quail to eat and water to drink, they still did not believe that they would be able to drive out the "giants" from their Promised Land. They allowed fear to paralyze them, and their small-minded thinking resulted in forty years of wandering in the wilderness.

Like the Israelites did so many years ago, many people nowadays are wandering through their own wildernesses because of their self-limiting beliefs and cynical mind-sets.

Like the Israelites did so many years ago, many people nowadays are wandering through their own wildernesses because of their self-limiting beliefs and cynical mind-sets. When they finally make the decision to cross over into their own Promised Lands, their fears, insecurities, and religious thinking do not automatically disappear. Like the Israelites, they have to drive them out.

DRIVING OUT WRONG THINKING

Religious thinking can be a major hindrance that keeps people from experiencing the promises of God. One religious belief that keeps many people out of their lands of abundance involves dwelling pessimistically on Job 1:21: *"The LORD gave, and the LORD hath taken away."* Ignoring the latter part of the verse, in which this faithful man of God, in spite of many tribulations, proclaimed, *"blessed be the name of the Lord,"* they focus on *"hath taken away"* and start seeing God as a vengeful Being who delights in removing sources of joy from their lives.

We can see the error of dwelling on this idea by looking at John 10:10, which reads, *"The thief cometh not, but for to steal, and to kill, and to destroy: I [Jesus] am come that they might have life, and that they might have it more abundantly,"* and at James 1:17, which assures us, *"Every good and perfect gift is from above, and cometh down from the Father of lights, with whom is no variableness, neither shadow of turning."*

In John 10:10, Jesus clearly distinguishes Himself from a thief. His desire is for all Christians to have full, abundant lives—lives filled with *"good and perfect"* gifts. Yet, many Christians give up on God when their lives are bombarded with disappointments and setbacks—job loss, the death of a loved one, a terminal illness, and so forth. They think, *God is supposed to give me "good things." What did I do to deserve all this trouble? He is either not omnipotent or not good; otherwise, He wouldn't let me suffer like this.* They become ensnared by this mind-set and tend to overlook or to misunderstand His intention of abundant life for them.

Abundant life isn't exclusively about life on earth. It doesn't mean that God promises that everyone will be "blessed," according to the world's definition of the term. Most people equate abundant life with prosperity, fame, leisure, and love—but what about people living in Third World countries who still describe their lives as "abundant"? An abundant life is filled with the joy of the Lord, which transcends socioeconomic status, wealth strata, age, race, ethnicity, health, and other factors typically used to assess "abundance." True abundance and joy are unconditional, for they spring from an everlasting and infinite Source: God the Father. And our joy will be complete only in heaven, a *"far better"* place to be (Philippians 1:23).

True abundance and joy are unconditional, for they spring from an everlasting and infinite Source: God the Father.

God is the author of all life. He does not take life; He gives it, but sin takes it from us. Death was never in the original plan for mankind, but it became part of mankind's inevitable destiny when Adam sinned in the garden of Eden.

The result of that sin is made clear in Romans 5:12: *"Wherefore, as by one man sin entered into the world, and death by sin; and so death passed upon all men, for that all have sinned."* You can see from this verse that God was not responsible for death—man was. God did not introduce sin into the world. But thanks be to God that He did not leave us in a state of automatic and inescapable condemnation!

Jesus came to the earth to redeem mankind back to God. He came to destroy the works of the devil in our lives and thus enable us to have abundant life, both here on earth, because we can be in relationship with Him, and ultimately in heaven, where we will fellowship with Him forever. Rightfully, we should be banished to hell when we die because of our transgressions. Yet our "abundant lives" will continue with unimaginable abundance in heaven, thanks to Jesus' sacrifice.

When you believe the lie that God punishes you with bad things, you will believe that sickness, death, and poverty come from Him as retribution for sinful deeds.

God does not promise a life without suffering. His own perfect Son, Jesus, suffered while He lived as a man; why do you, an imperfect human, expect immunity from it? Jesus told His disciples, *"In the world ye shall have tribulation"* (John 16:33). But He did not stop there and leave them despondent. Rather, He went on to assure them, *"Be of good cheer; I have overcome the world."* When problems and difficult situations come your way, do not turn your back on God and pout. Instead, call upon Him in times of distress, for He *"daily bears our burdens"* (Psalm 68:19 NIV). First Peter 5:7 exhorts you, *"Cast all your anxieties on him because he cares for you"* (NIV).

We see in the book of Ephesians that when Jesus was raised from the dead, *all things* were put under His feet. (See Ephesians 1:22.) Jesus won back the authority that Adam had handed over to Satan.

No longer are you dominated by the devil. When you choose to believe what the Bible says about you, you will realize that you are blessed in the city and blessed in the country. (See Deuteronomy 28:3.) You will understand that you are the head and not the tail, and that

God wants you to live above your circumstances rather than beneath them. (See verse 13.)

What Street Do You Live On?

God wants you to live a good life that is grounded in Him—a life where you are not struggling and living from paycheck to paycheck with barely enough money to get by, especially if this financial strain is due to an uncontrollable addiction to shopping, increasing your possessions, and other habits of materialism. Even though He said He will bless everything your hand touches (see Psalm 1:3), you are the one who will decide whether you will live at the corner of Barely Get By Street and Grumble Alley, or on the main straightaway of Shall Boulevard. The residents of Shall Boulevard live by this Scripture: "*Whosoever...shall not doubt in his heart, but shall believe that those things which he saith shall come to pass; he shall have whatsoever he saith*" (Mark 11:23).

If financial problems seem to dominate your life, it's time to think about moving to Shall Boulevard. The brochure about this street says:

The Lord is my Shepherd; I shall not want. (Psalm 23:1)

Surely goodness and mercy shall follow me all the days of my life. (Psalm 23:6)

I [shall] *say of the Lord, "You are my refuge and my fortress."* (Psalm 91:2)

I have made up my mind to live on Shall Boulevard, but I am not the only person who has an opportunity to live on this street. I have no mansion that monopolizes the space. In fact, Shall Boulevard is an endless street with a limitless capacity for new homes and residents, so you can live there, too. The only requirement for moving to Shall Boulevard is to align your words with God's Word and see yourself in the same way that God sees you.

He sees you as fearless (2 Timothy 1:7), He sees you as a conqueror (Romans 8:37), and He sees you as a victorious overcomer (1 John 5:4

AMP). How can you even think about defeat if these terms define your self-perception?

SPEAK TO YOUR MOUNTAIN

In Mark 11:23, Jesus said that with faith, we can move mountains—those seemingly insurmountable obstacles that keep us from accepting the promises of God.

> *Whoever says to this mountain, "Be removed and be cast into the sea," and does not doubt in his heart, but believes that those things he says will be done, he will have whatever he says.*
> (Mark 11:23 NKJV)

Unfortunately, too many Christians are not speaking to their mountains but are asking God to give them the strength to climb over them. He does not want you to climb mountains; He wants you to talk to them so that they can be cast into the sea.

CHANGING THE WAY YOU THINK

To people bound by religious thinking and self-limiting beliefs, the above Scripture probably means little. Even though God has provided ways out of their particular situations, they do not acknowledge this fact and sit still rather than act. For most of their lives, they have been singing the same dreary song, over and over, and they do not see how speaking the Word of God to a situation—especially if the situation is the size of a mountain—can change anything about it.

If you find yourself at the foot of a formidable mountain right now, it is likely that a lot of "religious" ideas and wrong thinking have been assimilated into your core belief system, where they are preventing you from receiving what God has promised you in His Word.

Jesus told the Jews who believed in Him, *"Ye shall know the truth, and the truth shall make you free"* (John 8:32). If you are so bound up with the status quo that you refuse to accept the truth of God's Word, what can help you?

To break free from your current lifestyle and move forward into abundance, you first have to change the way you think. When your mind-set has changed, your lifestyle will change accordingly.

Jesus gave us power to trample on serpents and scorpions; our power exceeds all power that the enemy possesses. (See Luke 10:19.) Yet, instead of claiming their authority in Christ and walking in it, many believers abide in weakness and inferiority, far below the level they can attain. Instead of believing the Word of God and affirming what God has said in His Word about them, they are moaning, crying, and whining.

Jesus gave us power to trample on serpents and scorpions; our power exceeds all power that the enemy possesses.

These people may come to church regularly and get built up by the minister, who explains to them how to live victoriously through the Word of God. They may get excited while sitting in the pews, but after the service, it's another story. When they exit the door of the church, they resume their familiar gripes: "I don't have enough money," "I cannot pay my bills," "I'll never be able to afford to repair my car," "I'll never get better."

The most important words in your vocabulary are the words that you say to yourself, about yourself. For that which you continually say becomes a part of your core belief system.

FROM FACT TO TRUTH

Your core belief system includes the principles, ethics, and values by which you order your life and make decisions. However, some aspects or features of your belief system were assimilated unconsciously, with little to no deliberate effort or sanction on your part.

Many of your beliefs were passed down to you from other people: your family members, friends, and college professors, for instance. Because these beliefs originated in people whom you trust, admire, and respect, you accepted them as absolute truth and absorbed them totally. Then, when you heard the truth of God's Word, instead of changing the way you were thinking, you rejected the truth of any Scriptures that conflicted with the "absolute truth" of your inherited beliefs. Rather than readjusting your own perspective, you changed or rejected God's Word.

It's as if your mind is a computer installed with antivirus software that blocks the Word of God. When the truth of God's Word "invades" your mind, the worldly antivirus program keeps it from getting past its security system and into your heart. You're "safe" from Scripture—to the peril of your soul.

If you continue to block out the truth of God's Word, you will perpetuate wrong beliefs, and you will experience the same things over and over again, without any hope of change.

James warned us to *"lie not against the truth"* (James 3:14). The Word of God is the ultimate truth, and all "facts" are subordinate to it.

For example, if you are married, it may be a *fact* that your marital relationship needs help. It may be a *fact* that your economic status is inadequate to take care of your financial needs. However, the *truth* of God's Word can change the facts in your life and even reverse them. Your marital relationship can improve and love can be restored. You can find a new job and earn enough money to pay off your debt.

WALKING IN THE LIGHT

The entrance of God's Word brings light into any situation. (See Psalm 119:130.) Before God's Word comes on the scene, our environment is dark, our vision obscured by shadows and dimness. When the Word of God sheds light on a situation, the entire place is transformed. Wisdom is granted; a new perspective is gained.

You have probably experienced a power outage at night caused by violent weather. A strong thunderstorm or blast of strong wind knocks the power lines away from a transformer, plunging the homes of you and your neighbors into darkness. When everything is dark, you are limited in what you can do. Even if you light candles or carry a flashlight, you cannot walk in the dark as easily as you did in the daylight or by the light of a lamp. You must step slowly and cautiously so that you will not bump into furniture or run into doorframes.

Spiritually speaking, the same is true when God's Word is not shining on a situation. You try walking in the darkness, but you keep stumbling and tripping over things. Obstacles hinder your progress, and without the enlightenment and wisdom of God's Word, you have no way of seeing them clearly or from His perspective. Thus, you have no way of knowing how to circumnavigate them.

Most people do not realize that they are walking in the dark. They keep stumbling, and the Bible calls this sin:

> *God is light, and in him is no darkness at all. If we say that we have fellowship with him, and walk in darkness, we lie, and do not the truth: but if we walk in the light, as he is in the light, we have fellowship one with another, and the blood of Jesus Christ his Son cleanseth us from all sin.* (1 John 1:5–7)

Any area of your life in which you resist God's Word will remain shrouded in utter darkness. God said that He did not give you a spirit of fear (see 2 Timothy 1:7), but when you allow yourself to be dominated by fear, you are walking in darkness; you have not allowed the light of God's Word and the power of His presence to illuminate your soul and dispel your fears. When you refuse to release— or forgive—someone who has wronged you, you are walking in darkness.

But when you receive the Word of God as truth and regard it as the final authority in all matters, you will find that it provides answers to all of your questions. Some people have stubborn wills. They refuse to forgive and thereby insist on remaining in strife. God's light will shine in their hearts once again, though, when they forgive others as God forgave them. As long as you are too stubborn to change, you will remain in your same decrepit state.

When you receive the Word of God as truth and regard it as the final authority in all matters, you will find that it provides answers to all of your questions.

You have a choice to make. If you want to walk in all that God has promised you, you will have to drive out the "ites" from your life—the personal issues and attitude problems that are keeping you from possessing all that God wants you to have. Remember the story of the salmon? You will have to imitate these fish and swim against the current that has been dragging you downstream in a direction you no longer want to travel.

If you are willing to come out of your comfort zone and leave your personal fears and self-limiting beliefs behind, giving them to God instead (see 1 Peter 5:7), God's Word will prevail in your life and enable you to enter—and remain in—your very own Promised Land.

Chapter 6

The Secret to True Success

Many books have been published explaining how to succeed in ventures such as business, real estate, and marriage. Each book offers "secrets" to success, but I have to wonder how something can be a secret if it's printed in book form for millions of readers to see. When we're all in on the same "secret," it isn't much of a secret, now, is it? I am going to let you in on a secret I have discovered: there are no secrets to success. None exists! Any "secrets" or tactics that assure success have all been uncovered in the Word of God. There are foolproof truths about success, but they're not for a select few; they are for everyone's knowledge and benefit. And they're found in the Bible, the very Word of God.

I am going to let you in on a secret I have discovered: there are no secrets to success.

I often say that the "secret to success" is not found in the *Wall Street Journal* but rather in Joshua 1:8. This verse describes what I consider to be the shortest distance between the points of desire and fulfillment, plan and procurement. Yet none of the principles found in this passage will work unless *you* work it. Success does not come automatically. It follows hard work and unflinching perseverance. The only place where *success* precedes *work* is in the dictionary. In reality, they are side-by-side.

MEDITATING ON THE WORD

> *This book of the law shall not depart out of thy mouth; but thou shalt meditate therein day and night, that thou mayest observe to do according to all that is written therein: for then thou shalt make thy way prosperous, and then thou shalt have good success.*
>
> (Joshua 1:8)

The *"book of the law"* refers to the first five books of the Bible, or the Pentateuch. This is also called the Law of Moses. Regardless of the terminology, it is the Word of God.

Joshua was instructed to *meditate* (ponder, think) on the Word. Why is this important? Meditation is the process by which Scripture becomes lodged in your heart. The Word of God ought to be the first and last thing you look at every day.

When you rise in the morning, make sure that you allow ample time to read your Bible and reflect on the truths taught therein. You may choose to read a chapter at a time, working your way through the Bible from start to finish. Or, you may allocate fifteen or twenty minutes and read as much as you can in that time. You may also do a topical study, choosing a particular book or theme to explore for a few days or weeks at a time. One good habit to practice, in addition to your regular reading, is to read a proverb a day. This way, you will start your day with the wisdom of God. Then, when you go to bed at night, make sure it isn't so late that you are too tired to read the Word.

The Word of God is your strength and your sustenance. Its truths and promises uphold you, day in and day out, through life's trials and triumphs alike. The devil will do everything in his power to get you sidetracked or to make your life so busy that you neglect the Word.

There is always enough time to read your Bible every day—you just need to find it. Incorporate Bible reading into your lunch hour. If your job allows you to take brief breaks in the morning and afternoon, instead of joining your coworkers in the cafeteria for a pity party spent complaining about management, overtime, and other job-related issues, separate yourself and build yourself up in the Word.

Take one Bible verse and read it over and over. Consider each key word and think about its meaning. Make the verse personal by replacing pronouns with your own name, if appropriate, or with the personal pronouns "I" or "me." The Psalms lend themselves well to this practice, and they will revolutionize your understanding of God's promises, making them real to you.

CHARTING A NEW COURSE

Notice also in Joshua 1:8 that God told Joshua to let the Word *"not depart out of thy mouth"*; he was to keep God's Word in his mouth at all times. To keep the Word continually means speaking things that are in line with Scripture. Instead of looking at a situation and speaking what you see, see what God sees and say it.

Joshua and Caleb both spoke forth God's Word when Moses sent them to spy out the Promised Land. They believed that God would enable them to "take" the land, in spite of all the "ites" who lived there (see Numbers 13:30) and the negative statements made by the other ten spies (see Numbers 13:27–29). Forty-five years later, the time that God determined that Israel would enter the Promised Land, Caleb was still speaking the Word when he said to Joshua, *"Give me this mountain"* (Joshua 14:12), referring to the one God had promised him all those years earlier.

You will never make it through adversity if you talk as if you won't. Your words have the capacity to be prophetic.

If you feel defeated in life, do not be like the ten spies whose dismal outlooks had defeated them before they could even try to win. Do not speak forth your defeat. Remember, these spies knew that God had promised to give them the land, and yet they chose to go by their senses, saying, "We are like grasshoppers in their sight." (See Numbers 13:33.) You will never make it through adversity if you talk as if you won't. Your words have the capacity to be prophetic.

Say that you are more than a conqueror through Jesus Christ who loves you. (See Romans 8:37.) Declare that you can do all things through Christ who strengthens you. (See Philippians 4:13.)

No matter what you see around you or how you feel, affirm what the Bible says. For example, if you sneeze, you shouldn't say, "Well, it is the start of cold and flu season. I am probably catching a cold." Instead, you should say, "Thank God I do not have to be dominated by sickness anymore. Through the stripes of Jesus, I can live in divine health." (See 1 Peter 2:24.)

If your budget is tight, do not lament your lack continually. When it looks as though you might not have enough money, say, "God has promised to meet all my needs according to His riches in glory." (See Philippians 4:19.) "He provides for the sparrow, and I know He will provide for me, as well." (See Matthew 6:26.)

Keep your mouth full of the Word of God. Joshua 1:8 says that when you do this, you will make your way prosperous. By meditating continually on Scripture, day and night, and speaking God's Word rather than the appearance of your circumstances, you will cast out negativity and fear and will ultimately change the course of your life.

A Couple's Faith in the Face of Fear

Fear is not selective; it affects everyone regardless of age, ethnicity, socioeconomic status, education, and other distinguishing characteristics. There was a young couple in our church who deeply desired to have children. Both husband and wife were ambitious, energetic, and well-positioned in promising careers. When they told us that they were expecting, we could see the joy beaming in their eyes.

However, within a few months of her pregnancy, the wife had a miscarriage. Their once joyous and proud faces now displayed sadness and fear. They felt anxious and uncertain about how to proceed now that their hopes for a family had been dashed.

My wife and I counseled the couple and discouraged them from growing bitter, angry, or sad. We reminded them to maintain their faith and trust God to grant them the desires of their hearts. This can be done confidently because of what the Bible promises us. Mark 11:24 says, *"Therefore I say to you, whatever things you ask when you pray, believe that you receive them, and you will have them"* (NKJV). Likewise, Psalm

37:4 assures us, *"Delight yourself also in the LORD, and He shall give you the desires of your heart"* (NKJV).

After a season of spiritual reflection and emotional encouragement, the couple had renewed their enthusiasm, and they determined to try again. There was great anticipation, especially when the wife became pregnant again. However, another miscarriage ensued.

At this point in their counseling, we encouraged them with the story of Hannah. (See 1 Samuel 1.) Hannah was despairing because her womb had been *"closed"* (verse 5 NKJV); she could not conceive. With diligence, she petitioned the Lord for a child. She poured out her heart to God in fervent prayer for a son, causing many people around her, including her husband and the priest, Eli, to think that she was drunk. But Hannah continued to pray and worship God, trusting Him and believing that He would bless her with the child she so greatly desired. (See verses 7–19.)

Sure enough, *"the LORD remembered her"* (verse 19), and Hannah conceived, giving birth to a son, Samuel, who would become a priest and prophet of the Lord. Later, Hannah went on to have three more sons and two daughters—her prayer was answered above and beyond her original hope! (See 1 Samuel 2:21.)

This biblical example lifted the couple's spirits. About a year later, the wife became pregnant again—this time with twins! Needless to say, this was a more-than-expected blessing for them. During the final trimester of her pregnancy, the wife's doctor performed a test, the results of which caused him to confine her to bed rest for the remainder of her pregnancy. This, paired with the tragic memories of her previous losses, opened a doorway in the woman's heart for doubt, fear, and anxiety to creep in. The couple called us and asked us to pray with them.

We did, reminding them that Scripture urges us to *"fight the good fight of faith"* (1 Timothy 6:12). This verse reveals the interesting truth that, often, an act of faith precipitates a "faith fight." But the fight of faith is a "good" fight because a good fight is one that you win! Knowing that Christ, who has overcome the world (see Romans 8:37), lives in us, and that nothing is too hard for Him (see Genesis 18:14), the couple's faith was strengthened.

Before the wife's pregnancy had gone full-term, the twins were delivered prematurely in an induced labor due to the doctors' concern for their chances of survival. They were placed in special units reserved for preemies, where they received round-the-clock care. One of the twins had to be put on a respirator.

My wife and I visited the couple at the hospital, and we encouraged them to resist the spirit of fear (see 2 Timothy 1:7), meditate on God's Word (see Psalm 119:11), realize that their fight is not with flesh and blood (see Ephesians 6:12), believe that God's benefits are good (see Psalm 103:2–10), and trust that He will make good on His promises (see Numbers 23:19). After studying these Scriptures, the couple was even more determined to trust God's Word and receive what He had promised them.

Today, the twins are excelling in all of their schoolwork and extracurricular activities. By dispelling fear, doubt, and worry, the couple created a faith-filled environment. Hebrews 11:6 states that *"without faith it is impossible to please [God]: for he that cometh to God must believe that he is, and that he is a rewarder of them that diligently seek him."* Their story is one of faith, perseverance, and victory in the face of crisis.

When you make a regular habit of putting the Word in first place on a daily basis, you will begin to experience greater success in receiving all that God's Word promises you.

NO AGE REQUIREMENT

The phrase *"day and night"* (Joshua 1:8) implies one day after another, with no gaps or breaks in between. To read the Word "day and night," then, means that you must make a regular, constant practice of reading and reflecting on God's Word.

When you make a regular habit of putting the Word in first place on a daily basis—not just on Wednesday nights at Bible study and Sunday mornings at church, but every day—you will begin to experience greater success in receiving all that God's Word promises you.

Joshua 1:8 was not written just to those who are twenty-one years of age and older, either. It was written to *all* believers, and whoever will follow the instructions found in this verse will reap great benefits.

There is no age requirement when it comes to the Word of God. If a young child reads Scripture or hears someone else read it to him and then does what it says, he will find its promises fulfilled in his life. The Word will work for senior citizens and teenagers just as well as it will work for middle-aged men and women. It will work for everyone who puts it to work in his or her life.

The Word is powerful and strong. When you read it, meditate on it, and speak it aloud and in your heart, it will change your life and your circumstances.

OPEN THE DOOR FOR BLESSINGS

Meditating on the Word is not something that will consume your entire day and leave no time for you to do anything else. If you cannot devote an hour each day to reading the Word, then start with ten or fifteen minutes. You probably spend more than fifteen minutes of every day reading the newspaper, surfing the Internet, or skimming e-mails. How much more important than these activities is the Word of God?

Maybe you are interested in sports, and each day, you visit ESPN.com or read the sports section in the local newspaper. If you can make time to catch up on sports scores and game results, then surely you can make time to read the Bible. Or perhaps you like getting a bargain by using coupons when you shop. If you have enough time to scan the newspaper for coupons for weekend sales at your favorite department stores, then you can find time to read the Word.

If people would read the Word of God with the same intensity and focus with which they read the daily paper, best-selling novels, and pop culture magazines, just think where their spiritual lives would be. Think of what they could overcome! When you give the Word the respect that it is due, you open the door to usher God's blessings into your life.

THE WISDOM OF GOD

The phrase *"have good success"* found in Joshua 1:8 literally means to deal wisely in the affairs of life.[1] When you think about this, it seems logical—you will be successful when you are wise in your daily affairs.

It is wise to remain faithful to your spouse and avoid the entanglement of adulterous affairs. It is wise to live within your means: an item may be on sale at a significantly reduced price, but that does not mean you have to buy it—especially if you do not have enough money.

It is wise for parents to discipline their children when they are young. Later, when the children have grown, they will be grateful that their parents cared enough to train them up in the way they should go. (See Proverbs 22:6.) And the parents will take pride in their children rather than feeling ashamed of their children's reckless actions. (See Proverbs 29:15, 17.)

Wise instruction for every area of life comes from the Word of God. If you experience a mishap or an episode of failure along the way, no matter your pursuit or place on the path, the Word is full of promises to let you know that God has already engineered your comeback.

WALKING IN DOMINION

Let's look again at Genesis 1:28, where God commanded Adam to *"be fruitful, and multiply, and replenish the earth, and subdue it: and have dominion over the fish of the sea, and over the fowl of the air, and over every living thing that moveth upon the earth."*

This mission is yours, too, and God wants you to succeed in fulfilling it. In order to do this, you must succeed in life—but not just for self-gratification or recognition by your fellow men. God wants you to live a full, meaningful, and purposeful life in which you are a blessing to others.

There is no blessing without the Word, for God's Word is the source of all blessings.

You see, your life is not all about you. It is about being a blessing to others, serving them with the love of Christ. (See Galatians 5:13; Colossians 3:17; Philippians 2:4.) It all starts with the Word. God's Word will enable you to bless people wherever you go because you will be sharing the blessings that you ushered into your life through the Scriptures. There is no blessing without the Word, for God's Word is the source of all blessings.

GOD KNOWS SOMETHING YOU DON'T KNOW

Another point we can learn from Joshua 1:8 is that your life becomes better only when you become better. When I counsel people who face extreme difficulties and impossible problems, I often hear them say, "I did everything I knew to do." Since their lives are in utter turmoil, "everything" they knew was evidently not enough; otherwise, they would not still find themselves in their difficult situations.

Allow me to pose a few questions to you. When you feel that you have done everything you know to do to remedy a situation, do you ever stop to wonder whether God knows even more things to do? Have you considered that God might know something that you do not? If God has more wisdom on the subject—and He always does—then you can tap into His wisdom. But how? The answer to these questions is very simple:

If any of you lack wisdom, let him ask of God, that giveth to all men liberally, and upbraideth not; and it shall be given him.

(James 1:5)

You can always go to God when you need help, knowing with complete assurance that He will never put you down for not knowing something. Throughout your life, you might have been called "dumb" or "stupid," but God will never condemn or chide you for lacking knowledge that you never had an opportunity to attain. In fact, it is His good pleasure to show you what to do and to help you in any situation.

People often arrive at impasses in their marriage relationships, business deals, child-raising techniques, and other significant life situations. Even when you have done everything you know to do, there is always more to learn, most obviously in stalemates that seem to offer no clear solution.

WHOM ARE YOU LEANING ON?

A quandary or confusing situation is no time to be stubborn and refuse to ask for help, especially from the God who created the universe.

When you have come to the end of your knowledge, lean on God. Lean on the One who knows everything.

People often come to their wits' ends in certain situations. They are frustrated because they have exhausted all of their conceivable options and think that there is nothing left to do.

In most cases, they have not even begun to tap into what God knows. When they find out what He knows—everything—and begin applying His knowledge to their lives and circumstances, everything changes. The Israelites are a perfect example:

> *The stormy wind...lifts up the waves of the sea. [Those aboard] mount up to the heavens, they go down again to the deeps; their courage melts away because of their plight. They reel to and fro and stagger like a drunken man and are at their wits' end [all their wisdom has come to nothing]. Then they cry to the Lord in their trouble, and He brings them out of their distresses.*
> (Psalm 107:25–28 AMP)

It is as simple as approaching God as your heavenly Father and asking Him, in the name of Jesus, for the solution to your situation. If you are concerned about your children, for instance, here is an example of how to pray for them:

> *Father, my children are not behaving in line with Your Word. I desire them to, but apparently there are some things I do not know. I am coming to You according to Your Word. You said that if any man lacks wisdom, You will give it to him. Father, I admit that I lack wisdom in how to deal with this situation. I need Your wisdom, Lord, and am confident that You will give it to me.*

It does not matter what type of problem you face. God has the answer and will show you what to do if you will ask Him.

Jesus said that whoever would come unto Him, He would *"in no wise cast out"* (John 6:37). The Bible harmonizes with itself. It does not say one thing in the Gospels and another thing in the Epistles. It is consistent from beginning to end. In the Epistles, the apostle Paul encouraged us to *"be careful for nothing; but in every thing by prayer and*

supplication with thanksgiving let your requests be made known unto God"
(Philippians 4:6).

God is omniscient, meaning that He is completely knowledgeable about everything that is, was, and ever will be. He knows what is on our minds even before we think it, but we are still to talk to God, telling Him what bothers us, what brings us joy, and so forth.

> *Is any among you afflicted? let him pray. Is any merry? let him
> sing psalms. Is any sick among you? let him call for the elders
> of the church; and let them pray over him, anointing him with
> oil in the name of the Lord: and the prayer of faith shall save the
> sick, and the Lord shall raise him up.*　　　(James 5:13–15)

A DIVINE INVITATION

In the Old Testament, God said, *"Come now, and let us reason together"* (Isaiah 1:18). The word *reason* in this verse means to present and argue your case.[2] Some people think that you argue only when you are angry with another person and disagree with what the individual is saying or doing. But another aspect of the word *argue* is to give reason for or against something, as in a court of law.

A lawyer defending an individual who has been accused of a crime and pleads "not guilty" will present before a judge and jury an argument to justify the defendant's actions as compliant with the law. On the other side is the prosecutor, who will present an argument to the contrary in an attempt to indict the defendant by proving his guilt to the jury.

We have all been summoned to the high court of heaven, where we can come before the throne of grace and receive help in times of need. (See Hebrews 4:16.) God has invited us to sit down and talk to Him, telling Him about what is troubling our minds or assaulting our bodies. We have this right of access to God through the blood of His Son.

God has invited us to sit down and talk to Him, telling Him about what is troubling our minds or assaulting our bodies.

Having therefore, brethren, boldness to enter into the holiest by the blood of Jesus, by a new and living way, which he hath consecrated for us, through the veil, that is to say, his flesh; and having an high priest over the house of God; let us draw near with a true heart in full assurance of faith. (Hebrews 10:19–22)

When we come into God's presence in our times of need, He will give us the wisdom we require and our lives will improve.

We need to think in terms of improvement. If you think that you have already arrived at the pinnacle of your potential, you will have no desire to do anything different from what you are doing or have done. This sort of complacency is a problem among many people. They think that they have done everything there is to do, and no one can convince them otherwise.

Those who adopt this attitude of indolence have parked themselves in a rut, not realizing that a rut is really a grave with both ends knocked out of it! None of us has arrived, and we will not arrive at our potential without God's help. We do not know all the answers, but Jesus does.

Room for Improvement

When some people reach the age of forty, fifty, or even sixty, they think that they have done everything there is to do in life. They believe that their best years are behind them and see little left to do or to be while they remain on earth.

This erroneous attitude is from the depths of hell. To think in this way is to lie to yourself. Who says that you cannot pursue an idea, start a business, or obtain a higher degree at age forty, fifty, sixty, seventy, eighty, or even ninety? If you adhere to this mind-set, your drive will become set like concrete, and you will be stuck with no hope of moving forward.

This type of mind-set is brought on largely by those to whom you have been listening. The people around you might have the fatalistic assumption that because they were born and raised in a certain neighborhood, they are destined to die in that very same neighborhood. If you live in that neighborhood, too, you might think that because of your family heritage, you have no hope of changing and breaking away from a predetermined pattern of life.

These words, however, contradict what God says and what the Bible teaches. God thinks of you and your future in this manner:

For I know the thoughts and plans that I have for you, says the Lord, thoughts and plans for welfare and peace and not for evil, to give you hope in your final outcome. (Jeremiah 29:11 AMP)

God desires to see all areas of your life become progressively better. How can you improve your public poise? Your education level? Your moral standards? How can you improve your service to God and to others? What about your job? Is there any way to improve your relationships with other people?

When a problem looks as large as a mountain, it seems immovable and impossible to solve. What would happen if you began making incremental adjustments in the areas that I mentioned above, as well as in others that you may identify? How would your life change? Dramatically. Sometimes, it takes only a slight adjustment to make a big difference.

AIMING FOR THE DESTINATION

Let me explain this further by giving you a lesson in space travel. On July 16, 1969, the Apollo 11 spacecraft was launched from the Kennedy Space Center in Cape Canaveral, Florida. It was the first manned mission to the moon. But when the craft was launched, it was not aimed at the moon's location on that day. Rather, it was aimed at the location where the moon *would* be on July 19, the day their rendezvous was projected.

The moon completes an elliptical orbit around the earth every thirty days. Because the moon follows an identical path each month, scientists can easily determine the exact location of the moon at any time, both present and future.

This explains why the spacecraft had to aim for a place where the moon wasn't—at least not yet. If your perspective permitted you a view of both outer space and the launchpad during liftoff, you would have thought that Apollo 11 was headed in the wrong direction. But the opposite was true: it was headed exactly where it needed to go, and on July 20, 1969, Commander Neil Armstrong put the first footprint on the moon's surface.

For the spacecraft to reach the moon at the proper time, the calculations determining its course had to be precise. The crew could not afford to be off by even a few degrees.

The distance between the earth and the moon is approximately 270,000 miles, and the spacecraft traveled approximately 25,000 miles an hour. Had their calculations been off by two degrees, Apollo 11 would not have been anywhere near the moon on July 19, 1969.

The same thing happens in our lives. At a young age, most of us were encouraged by parents and teachers to develop dreams that we wanted to accomplish in our lifetimes. But many of us grow up to miss the mark—we failed to take certain factors into account when making our calculations, and we ended up aiming for the wrong thing or heading in the wrong direction. Many people dream about the things they want to achieve but end up abandoning them altogether, long before they can even be launched.

We must aim for where we want to be and calculate how to get there, or we will wind up far off course.

As time passes and we look back at what we have accomplished in life, we often think, *I thought I would have been further along than I am right now.* After ten years have gone by, and then twenty and forty years, it becomes clear how far off course we have strayed. We must aim for where we want to be and calculate how to get there, or we will wind up far off course.

MAKING MIDCOURSE CORRECTIONS

When astronauts are traveling in outer space, they must check their instruments constantly and monitor their course closely. If they stray from the designated path, they must make midcourse corrections.

In fact, they may have to make hundreds of these corrections in a single day to ensure that they reach their destination.

If we, too, would learn to make midcourse corrections throughout our lives, we would be guaranteed to hit the marks for which we aim.

Picture a person who didn't think that running with a certain crowd would affect the course of his life in an adverse manner. He thought that his friends were cool. Even though his parents did not like them, he believed he knew better and would not heed their disapproval. The next thing he knew, he had a criminal record. He was charged with a variety of misdemeanors and petty crimes. Then, he was pulled over for a speeding violation and the police officer found illegal substances hidden in his trunk. Now, he faces a prison sentence and hefty prosecution.

His parents can be compared to NASA's Mission Control Center in Houston, Texas. They were trying to get him to make a midcourse correction in his early years. They were trying to warn him about debris that was coming across his path because of the company he kept and the things he became involved with. They wanted to help him to avoid the troubles that would ensue.

It was obvious to them that he was going off course. They knew that if he did not steer clear of the debris, he would lose "oxygen." They saw that he was, in effect, on the verge of losing fuel, without which he would not reach his destiny.

Then, one day—and that day always comes—he took a look around and discovered that he was floating somewhere in outer space with no clue how he got there. Nothing looked familiar. It was not where he wanted to be. And he had no idea how to get back on course.

HITTING THE MARK

Success does not come without sacrifice. You have to be willing to pay the price. You have to resolve to do whatever it takes—as long as it's scriptural and moral—to accomplish your goals and dreams. This will necessitate seizing the time.

Many people do not take charge of their time. We are told to redeem the time because the days are evil. (See Ephesians 5:16.) This means that we should make the best use of our time by ordering our priorities and spending our time accordingly.

It is easy to get caught up in socializing with friends, traveling to new places, and learning new things, which may cause you to veer off the path to your destiny and keep you from fulfilling your dreams. While there is a place for social interaction, too much fellowship with friends, relatives, and coworkers can be counterproductive in the process of fulfilling the will and purpose of God for your life.

At the end of his life, the apostle Paul was able to say, *"I have fought a good fight, I have finished my course, I have kept the faith"* (2 Timothy 4:7). He was able to make this proclamation because he had been focused throughout life's tests and trials. He had learned how to prioritize his time and did not permit himself to become distracted by anything that would take him off course.

To experience success in all areas of life—such as your career, your marriage, your education, and your health—you must think in terms of improvement. If you have been acting in a certain way for so long that your tendency to stray off course is automatic, do not despair; it is still possible to change this tendency.

BE STRONG AND COURAGEOUS

Getting back on course in order to live a victorious life requires you to develop and refine two traits: strength—which is closely akin to endurance and perseverance—and courage. Contrary to common belief, courage is not the absence of fear, but rather the ability to advance in the face of fear.

Courage is not the absence of fear, but rather the ability to advance in the face of fear.

It will take strength and courage on your part to look for a new set of friends if your current cronies are hindering you from fulfilling your destiny. It will take courage to resist doing the same things you have always done—those familiar, comfortable, yet counterproductive habits—and to step out in a new direction.

When the Lord chose Joshua to lead the children of Israel into the Promised Land, He had to encourage the newly appointed leader. In fact, He strongly commanded Joshua three times in the first chapter of the book of Joshua to be strong and of good courage:

> *There shall not any man be able to stand before thee all the days of thy life: as I was with Moses, so I will be with thee: I will not fail thee, nor forsake thee. Be strong and of a good courage: for unto this people shalt thou divide for an inheritance the land, which I sware unto their fathers to give them. Only be thou strong and very courageous, that thou mayest observe to do according to all the law, which Moses my servant commanded thee: turn not from it to the right hand or to the left, that thou mayest prosper withersoever thou goest.....Have not I commanded thee? Be strong and of a good courage; be not afraid, neither be thou dismayed: for the LORD thy God is with thee whithersoever thou goest.* (Joshua 1:5–7, 9)

As you endeavor to make the necessary midcourse adjustments, as Joshua did, be strong and of good courage. God is with you every step of your journey, and He desires for you to reach your destiny. In the same way that He was with Joshua, He will be with you. He will not fail you, for He is faithful to fulfill His promises.

Chapter 7

Thoughts, Words, and Actions

When Jesus began His earthly ministry, the first message He preached after coming into Galilee addressed the way people thought. I believe that He chose to address the subject of thinking because almost everything in our lives and experiences has, in one sense, been created by our own thinking, for better or for worse.

You are the steward over all that is in your conscious mind. What you think about and dwell on eventually becomes what you believe. What you believe determines what you speak, and you will have what you say. Thus, thoughts determine what you have. It is a chain reaction.

In the book of Proverbs, we read, *"For as* [man] *thinketh in his heart, so is he"* (Proverbs 23:7). It is only reasonable to conclude from this verse that you cannot have a negative mind-set and lead a positive life. The inverse is also true: you cannot lead a positive life and entertain a negative mind-set at the same time. The two are mutually exclusive.

If your mind is filled with negativity, you will experience constant anger, bitterness, and frustration.

If your mind is filled with negativity, you will experience constant anger, bitterness, and frustration. When your thoughts are filled with negativity, your words will also be filled with negativity, and negative words can hardly produce positive outcomes.

Nothing will ever work out right for you, if that's what you believe. You will find a worm in every apple and a thorn on every flower. It is impossible for you to lead a positive lifestyle if you are filled with so many negatives.

Another way to read Proverbs 23:7 is, "As it goes on the inside of you, so will it go on the outside." The point is that you are not *who* you think you are; *how* you think is who you are. Everything you have and the position you hold in life are the result of the way in which you think.

That was the essence of Jesus' first message in Galilee after His temptation in the wilderness by the devil. (See Matthew 4:1–16.) When Jesus heard that His cousin John had been thrown into prison, He went to Galilee and began His message with these words: *"Repent: for the kingdom of heaven is at hand"* (Matthew 4:17).

The word *repent* means "to change one's mind,"[1] or to change one's way of thinking. If your thinking can change, your entire life can change, because your life will travel in the direction of your most dominant thoughts.

Repent also means to turn from sin and dedicate oneself to the amendment of one's life. Again, change is involved, for turning implies a change in direction.

Even though your thoughts are intangible, they are very real things that involve two categories: physical and spiritual. We can see the distinguishing line between physical and spiritual things in 2 Corinthians 4:18:

While we look not at the things which are seen, but at the things which are not seen: for the things which are seen are temporal; but the things which are not seen are eternal.

This verse attests that things exist that cannot be seen or perceived with the natural senses, such as wisdom, truth, righteousness, and so forth.

THE UNSEEN REALM

There is an unseen realm that is physical. All matter is composed of atoms—microscopic entities whose subatomic particles—protons, neutrons, and electrons—react and interact in complex ways. Our bodies breathe, metabolize food, fight germs, and do other amazing yet everyday feats, all of which are performed at the microscopic level, which, although not visible to the naked eye, is no less real than your arms, legs, and other apparent parts.

Another good illustration of something you cannot see that has a significant impact on your life is radio waves. These invisible waves of energy transmit sound and information through the air so that you can listen to music and hear news reports or sporting event coverage on the radio. Our physical senses cannot see or hear a radio broadcast as it is travelling through the air; yet, at any given moment, millions of people have their radios tuned in to a particular frequency so that they can hear their favorite music or radio talk show. You cannot see the electromagnetic waves of a radio broadcast, but their invisibility does not disprove their presence. Turn your radio to a specific frequency, and you will hear what you cannot see.

Just because you cannot see radio waves does not mean that they do not exist. And just because you cannot see them does not mean that they are not real or that they do not have an impact on humanity.

ARE YOU TUNED IN?

In the same way that there are some very real natural things that are invisible to the human eye, there is also a very real spiritual world. God is broadcasting from the spiritual realm all the time; but, like a radio, you must be tuned in to the proper frequency to hear what He is broadcasting.

Are you catching the leadings of the Holy Spirit? Do you have the right antenna to pick up clear direction from God? The network from which God broadcasts is the All Things Are Possible Network.

However, you will not be able to receive clear sound if you are not tuned in to the right frequency.

Lest you think that you do not have the necessary equipment to tune in to the spirit realm, let's read where the Bible says that you do. According to Romans 12:3, God gives to every person a measure of faith; and it is through faith that we are able to perceive those things that are not seen. *"Faith is the substance of things hoped for, the evidence of things not seen"* (Hebrews 11:1). Note that this verse calls faith a *"substance"*—something real and substantial, albeit unseen.

You could say that faith is our sixth sense. It enables us to perceive, deal with, impact, appropriate, move, and draw upon the things that we are not able to see with our five physical senses. The things that are seen are what give us a hard time. They include the amount of money in our checkbooks, the rebellion of wayward children, and sicknesses in our bodies, among other things.

Yet these things can be undone, loosened, dissolved, suspended, and put out altogether by the things that we cannot see. In fact, the things that are not seen are, by their very nature, greater than the things that are seen.

CREATING WITH WORDS

Hebrews 11:3 says, *"Through faith we understand that the worlds were framed by the word of God, so that things which are seen were not made of things which do appear."*

Have you ever wondered how God created the heavens and the earth? If, before the world existed, there was but vast nothingness, what did God use to create the earth? He created the earth through things that are not perceivable through our five physical senses. He created the universe through His words.

When we learned earlier that we were created in the image and likeness of God (see Genesis 1:26), we learned, in essence, that God wants us to be as He is. By that, I mean that we are to act like God. In the same way that He created the world with His words, we are to create our worlds with our words.

The words that you speak in your household release powerful forces. They release things that may or may not be perceivable by your physical senses, but if you keep saying them long enough, you can eventually see the manifestation of what you are saying.

The words that you speak in your household release powerful forces.

For example, if the head of the household comes home from work and says day after day, "Nobody can get along in this house," those words will eventually come to pass. As the head of the household, this person holds a position of authority; whatever he or she says goes.

If the head of the house continually says things like, "We cannot seem to keep any money in this house," "Things are constantly breaking," or "Something always needs to be fixed around here," what is happening? A world is being created by the spoken word.

The Power of the Spoken Word

Take a look at two Bible verses that reinforce this idea. *"For by thy words thou shalt be justified, and by thy words thou shalt be condemned"* (Matthew 12:37). The *Amplified Bible* translates this verse as, *"For by your words you will be justified and acquitted, and by your words you will be condemned and sentenced."*

Proverbs 18:21 says, *"Death and life are in the power of the tongue: and they that love it shall eat the fruit thereof."* Can you see that words have the power to administer life and death?

Now, this does not mean that when you speak words of "death" to someone, he or she will drop dead. What it means is that you are either going to minister life into an environment or you are going to minister death into that environment. When you continually speak negative words about yourself, your job, your environment, your family, or anything else, your negative words can eventually prove to be self-fulfilling prophecies.

Some people wonder why bad things keep happening to them. If they would stop for a moment and listen to what they are saying, they would understand why their lives are plagued with problems.

In Matthew 4:17, when Jesus told the people to *"repent,"* He wanted them to change their ways of thinking. The apostle Paul offered us good advice about how to do this.

> *Finally, brethren, whatsoever things are true, whatsoever things are honest, whatsoever things are just, whatsoever things are pure, whatsoever things are lovely, whatsoever things are of good report; if there be any virtue, and if there be any praise, think on these things.*
>
> (Philippians 4:8)

Wrong thinking leads to wrong beliefs, and wrong beliefs lead to wrong words being spoken and, ultimately, to wrong actions.

We are the custodians of our thought lives. We are responsible for what we allow our minds to absorb and meditate on. Remember, a chain reaction connects thoughts to words to results. Wrong thinking leads to wrong beliefs, and wrong beliefs lead to wrong words being spoken and, ultimately, to wrong actions.

The apostle Paul instructed us to "[cast] *down imaginations, and every high thing that exalteth itself against the knowledge of God, and* [bring] *into captivity every thought to the obedience of Christ"* (2 Corinthians 10:5).

Every time a thought comes to your mind that is contrary to the Word of God, it is imperative for you to cast it down and force your mind to think instead on those things that are true, honest, just, pure, lovely, and of good report.

When you think on what is good and true, good beliefs, words, and actions will follow.

CHANGED MIND, CHANGED BODY

An example of this is found in the story of the woman with the issue of blood. (See Matthew 9:20–22.) She had exhausted all natural methods of healing that were available to her at that time. When she heard about Jesus, this ailing woman gained new hope that her situation could change—and that she could be healed.

Once her mind-set changed, her words followed her beliefs. In her brief encounter with Jesus, she received what she had so desperately sought for many years: healing.

And a certain woman, which had an issue of blood twelve years, and had suffered many things of many physicians, and had spent all that she had, and was nothing bettered, but rather grew worse, when she had heard of Jesus, came in the press behind, and touched his garment. For she said, If I may touch but his clothes, I shall be whole. And straightway the fountain of her blood was dried up; and she felt in her body that she was healed of that plague. And Jesus, immediately knowing in himself that virtue had gone out of him, turned him about in the press, and said, Who touched my clothes? And his disciples said unto him, Thou seest the multitude thronging thee, and sayest thou, Who touched me? And he looked round about to see her that had done this thing. But the woman fearing and trembling, knowing what was done in her, came and fell down before him, and told him all the truth. And he said unto her, Daughter, thy faith hath made thee whole; go in peace, and be whole of thy plague.

(Mark 5:25–34)

Very little biographical information is provided about this woman to help us relate to her. We don't know her marital status, source of income, family lineage, or social standing, yet we can draw several conclusions about her life.

We see that she had a problem. In her case, it was a physical issue. People can relate to her easily because most people have "issues"; and, like the woman whose bleeding had been a problem for twelve years, they have had to deal with their problems for long periods of time.

This woman was proactive in her efforts to seek relief from her issue to the point that she had exhausted all of her possibilities and resources. The Bible tells us in verse 26 that she had spent all of her money at the hands of many different physicians, but she did not get any better. In fact, she only got worse.

Often, when someone gets stuck in a difficult situation for a long period of time, he begins to lose hope. He exhausts all of his options and empties his bank account, yet nothing changes. He feels hopeless and helpless. What starkly penetrates through this woman's experience and reveals her true determination is the fact that instead of losing all hope, she kept on going, all the way to the Hope of hope: Jesus Christ.

THE STEP OF FAITH

Something dramatic happened to this woman because she heard of Jesus. (See Matthew 5:27.) No doubt, she had heard about all of the miraculous healings that Jesus had performed on people, some of whose situations were just as dire as hers. This woman, however, did what many people in hopeless situations fail to do. She took action.

Many people in the same situation would have stayed home when they heard about Jesus. They would have kept on saying, "My situation is hopeless. I have gone to every doctor around. What can Jesus do for me? I'll probably bleed to death."

Not this woman. She was determined to change her fate. She did not allow anything to deter her from coming in contact with Jesus. She decided that He was the solution to her problem, and she was resolved to do whatever it took to press through the crowd and touch the hem of His garment.

She stepped out in faith, and her words followed what she believed when she said to herself, *"If I may touch but his clothes, I shall be whole"* (verse 28).

Hers was a remarkably simple action—touching His garment— but an action born of a persistent mind-set. Having persevered through what must have been an embarrassingly difficult physical challenge, as well as pressing through a large throng of people, this courageous woman broke through to touch the Source of her deliverance.

When she first heard about Jesus, she stopped believing that her situation was hopeless. When she changed her mind, she changed what she said. She now believed that she could be well, and she said so with her mouth. When her beliefs changed, her actions followed suit.

When she touched Jesus' garment, a miraculous transaction occurred. Jesus felt *"virtue"* (*"power"* NIV) leave His body; simultaneously, the woman felt His healing power enter her body. (See verses 29–30.) Knowing that the woman's faith had drawn out His power, Jesus credited her faith for her miraculous healing. (See verse 34.) This account underscores the pleasure God receives when genuine faith in His Word is released. (See Hebrews 11:6.)

When a situation arises that seems impossible, instead of being dominated by fear, worry, and doubt, you must force your thoughts and beliefs to rest on the goodness of God and on the assurance that He will deliver you. Instead of speaking a negative end result to your circumstances, declare the Word of God. When you hold steadfastly to your confession and trust in God's Word, eventually your situation can turn around for the better instead of the worse.

> *When a situation arises that seems impossible, instead of being dominated by fear, worry, and doubt, you must force your thoughts and beliefs to rest on the goodness of God and on the assurance that He will deliver you.*

REMOVING THE "IF ONLY'S"

Do you see your situation as something that can change? Or do you think that you have to remain exactly as you are? Do you feel that you have made so many mistakes that you have lost all hope for a better future?

Life can be filled with many regrets, but if you want to move beyond the pain of your mistakes, you must change the way you speak and modify what you say.

How many times have you said, "My life would be a lot better if I had only…"? Until you get over the past issues in your life, your future will remain a prisoner of your past. You cannot step forward into the future when you are chained to the past.

For example, you might say, "If only I had not married that person"; "If only I had not done this or that." You have to move beyond past offenses, past mistakes, past failures, past broken marriages, past marital problems, past words that created bad blood, and past anything else that is holding you back. The list of these issues can be endless, but their hindering effects need not be.

I have seen fear creep into the life of an expectant mother whose past miscarriages started to persuade her that this pregnancy would also end in tragedy. But through the spoken Word, prayer, and the mighty power of the Holy Spirit, this woman gave birth to twins. Again, my wife and I joined the happy young couple in beholding this miracle. Today, those twins are enjoying the thrills of grade school. Praise God for His goodness!

Another woman required an urgent surgical procedure that involved the risk of paralysis. Dwelling on a family history, this woman allowed fear to work feverishly and nearly convince her that she would be paralyzed or, worse in her mind, never enjoy her new marriage or bear children. But God again showed Himself strong through the counsel of His Word and the power of His anointing. Today, that young woman is enjoying a wonderful marriage, has a healthy baby, and is pursuing her dream.

As long as you stay parked in the past, your present is useless and your future is inaccessible.

It is time to remove all of your "if only's." As long as you stay parked in the past, your present is useless and your future is inaccessible. You cannot undo anything that already has happened, but you can cast off the shackles of past problems and turn the page to start a new and more promising chapter.

Letting Go of the Past

Do not waste your time, energy, and mind power dwelling on traumatic events that took place in your past. I know that this can be more easily said than done. For some people, dwelling on the past can become like an addictive narcotic.

Often, those who talk constantly about their pasts, their mistakes, and the wrongs that have been done to them receive a lot of attention from others. Well-wishers smother them with sympathy, and some people find comfort in this attention. It becomes a self-perpetuating cycle of complaining—even if it means searching for something to complain about—and soaking up sympathy.

Take an honest look at yourself and examine your motives to see whether you are a person who seeks attention and dredges up painful experiences just for the purpose of drawing such attention to yourself.

If this is true, before long, you will be caught in a self-defeating cycle. You will find that you are constantly thinking about your past and continually speaking about your regrets, as well as lamenting all of the wrongs that have been done to you.

This practice goes against the Word of God, which instructs you regarding what to think about and how to speak. If you claim to believe God's Word but do not live according to it, you are not a doer of the Word, and you deceive yourself. (See James 1:23–25.) Bringing up past pains will not make you feel better. The sympathy and attention it earns you will provide only temporary comfort, if that. You will dig deeper and deeper into despair if you learn to dwell on misfortune and rely on the sympathy of others to support you.

You are the gatekeeper and guardian of your soul. It is up to you to cast down wrong thoughts (see 2 Corinthians 10:5) and to think on what is good and lovely (see Philippians 4:8). It is up to you to frame your future with words of faith.

You cannot use the excuse "I just can't help it." Who is in charge of your life? You, or your past? Learn from your past, but do not lean on it or live in it. Do not keep returning there. Get over the hurts and wrongs that were done to you, forgive those who may have been responsible, and forge a new future for yourself.

Learn from your past, but do not lean on it or live in it.

You can get over past regrets and hurts. They do not have to keep you from experiencing a bright future, especially when God has promised one to you. (See Jeremiah 29:11.)

A LESSON FROM THE ELEPHANT

A circus elephant is trained from a young age. Its ankle is shackled, then secured with a heavy chain that is attached to a stake in the ground. When the young elephant walks, it is limited by the length of the chain to an area with a specific circumference around the stake. No matter how hard the animal may yank and pull at the chain, it cannot go beyond the distance allowed by the chain, for it has not yet developed adequate bulk and strength to break loose.

Being bound like this for months, the young elephant eventually learns that it can move only a certain distance from the stake. Once the elephant has grown accustomed to being bound and staying within a certain area, the chain ceases to be necessary. The circus trainer has only to tie a slender rope around the enormous creature's ankle to mimic the feel of the shackle, thus keeping the elephant in its bounds. When the elephant is fully grown, it has more than adequate strength to rip out the stake, but because it has come to learn and accept its boundaries, it won't even try to escape. In the mind of the elephant, it can go no further. It has been conditioned to believe what is, in essence, a lie—that its strength is inadequate and that the area in which it is kept cannot be breached.

What lies are you listening to that have held you back your entire life? What fears and self-limiting beliefs have shackled you to your past? What negative words have you heard so often that you do not believe the truth about yourself—that you can do all things through Christ? (See Philippians 4:13.) What keeps you from believing that your life *will* amount to something?

Are you going to allow yourself to be limited by a lie, or are you going to break free from what is holding you in bondage?

ESSENTIAL CONDITIONS FOR CHANGE

The way to break free from the past is what I call the "essential conditions for change." Three things must be in place for you to experience life change.

1. First, you must *want change.*

You cannot keep rationalizing your anger. You cannot keep recalling past issues and attaching yourself to them. As long as you do these things, your life will not change for the better.

Mark 11:24 says, *"What things soever ye desire, when ye pray, believe that ye receive them, and ye shall have them."* Change will occur only if you earnestly desire it and present your desire prayerfully to God.

2. Second, you must be *willing to change.*

You have to be willing to turn your desire into action. If you desire better health, you must be willing to stop smoking, stop drinking excessive amounts of alcohol, stop using drugs, stop overeating, and stop any other harmful habits that you may practice. If you are overweight, for example, you have to be willing to give up doughnuts, muffins, and cheesecake—at least on a daily basis. You must be prepared to limit your consumption of fattening foods and prepare yourself to start an exercise plan. You must decide that the benefits of improved health far outweigh the disappointment and withdrawal of cutting calories and following a stricter diet.

3. Third, you must *make an effort to change.*

You cannot keep doing the same things over and over and expect your life to change. Start by changing the way you think and speak, then change your actions and routine. Begin doing something differently so you will get different results. This may necessitate enrolling in a college course to gain knowledge in an area, joining a local gym where you can exercise regularly, or attending a series of meetings with your local Alcoholics Anonymous chapter. Some of the changes you must make will not be easy, but I want you to realize that they are possible, and with God's help, you can undergo any change with great success.

As you begin to do the things that I have outlined in this book, you will see changes take place in your life. Keep in mind that it has taken you years to become who you are right now, so you must be willing to give the process for change your best effort and your utmost patience. Don't expect change overnight, but persevere through the process, however long it may take.

Once you begin down this path, leave no roads for retreat from your desired objective. Remember, you are today who you have always been; if you want to do something you have never done, though, you have to become somebody you have never been.

Chapter 8

It's All in the Math

The point of these teachings and Scriptures has been to help you understand how to overcome, because success is for everyone—and that means you, too. Never forget that God wants you to succeed in everything He has called you to do. And that truth alone is cause for rejoicing!

You don't have to wait for the "perfect" conditions before starting to apply God's wisdom to your life. If you delay, you may never begin the process of life change!

The following is a spiritual mathematical equation that you can use to calculate your potential for success, based on your application of everything we have discussed so far. You will notice that it has a common denominator, attitude, which, if positive, can be a catalyst for successful living. A negative attitude, on the other hand, tends to extinguish successful living.

This equation is not so much a computation as it is an illustrative guide for the manifestation of wholeness in every area of your life. As you work out this winning formula, remember that the key to it is like swimming upstream with the salmon—it's consistency. You need to be consistent in doing it.

As you begin to apply these positive actions in your life, you can expect to end up with a positive outcome. Keep your attitude

Expect to see improvement happen in your life, and you will—sooner than you think.

high where the things of God are concerned. Always try to be upbeat. Maintain enthusiasm. Cultivate a positive attitude and expect to make a change. Expect to see improvement happen in your life, and you will—sooner than you think. When your attitude is not contingent upon your circumstances and *"the joy of the LORD is your strength"* (Nehemiah 8:10), you will have unconditional joy that will not diminish even when your ego is deflated, your pride is cut down, and your plans fall through. These things won't faze you, and you will maintain a positive attitude to weather life's storms and secure future successes. (See 2 Corinthians 4:8–9, 16–18.) You can be *"sorrowful, yet alway rejoicing"* (2 Corinthians 6:10), as was the apostle Paul.

THE WINNING FORMULA

NA	*natural abilities*
L	*learned abilities*
E	*experiential knowledge*
D	*developed abilities*
A	*attitude*
LED	*sum of attributes and abilities acquired throughout life*
LEDA	*sum of the attributes and abilities that you have learned, experienced, and developed throughout your life, along with the attitude with which you acquired them*
IPC	*individual performance level*

NA is the measure of your natural abilities. These are the skills and attributes you were born with or are naturally inclined to exhibit. Many of these abilities were determined by your DNA—your genetic makeup, the unique blend of characteristics you received from your parents.

LED encompasses the attributes and abilities that you have acquired throughout life. To LED, we add A (attitude) to create the following acronym:

L—Learned

E—Experienced

D—Developed

A—Attitude

LEDA encompasses the attributes and abilities that you have learned, experienced, and developed throughout your life, along with the attitude with which you acquired them.

The spiritual equation works like this:

NA + LED x A = IPC

NA (your natural abilities) plus LED (your learned, experienced, and developed abilities), multiplied by A (your attitude), equals IPC (your individual performance level).

Your life is not a hopeless situation because you are in control of two of these factors. You control your LED (learned, experienced, and developed abilities), as well as your attitude.

The most important part of the equation by far is your attitude, for by this factor, your abilities are multiplied. The more positive your attitude and the greater its value, the greater the multiplier and the higher the outcome. This is why you can have a winning basketball team that has some natural abilities but has never developed all of the top-notch skills that most teams need in order to win. What puts them over the top and enables them to win a championship is their collective attitude.

We see many mediocre teams rise to the top with the right attitude. This has happened time and again.

On the other hand, you can have a team that has everything going for it—the best athletes, the most strategic plays—but somewhere along the line, the players develop a bad attitude of complacency and negativity. Once this happens, they set themselves up for defeat.

Your attitude will affect your IPC, positively or negatively. If you have a positive attitude, your IPC will be positive; conversely, a negative attitude will cause your IPC to be negative. The rules of algebra still apply.

A POSITIVE OUTCOME

Spiritually speaking, there are benefits that you can acquire from living a Christian lifestyle characterized by Bible study, prayer, church attendance, and participation in church events and outreach. These activities contribute to your relationship with God and also provide you with opportunities to be a blessing to others.

Your attitude determines the outcomes of your activities.

A key factor in determining your spiritual outcomes, as well as the degree to which you bless others, is your attitude. You can be in church every Sunday morning, attend every conference your church organizes, and read your Bible morning and night; but if you have a bad attitude, begin to murmur and complain, and allow self-limiting beliefs and criticisms to control your life, then you won't change. Your life will remain the same. Your attitude determines the outcomes of your activities.

This equation is valid in the life of every individual. Some people have more natural abilities than others, but that is not what is important to your success. Abilities can be learned, but often with limitations. Attitude, on the other hand, is personal, unique, and unlimited—it can be 100 percent positive and high enough to push someone with few abilities to exceed the success of someone who is highly skilled but has a lousy, pessimistic attitude.

Notice what it says in 2 Peter 1:4–7:

Whereby are given unto us exceeding great and precious promises: that by these ye might be partakers of the divine nature, having escaped the corruption that is in the world through lust. And beside this, giving all diligence, add to your faith virtue; and to virtue knowledge; and to knowledge temperance; and to temperance patience; and to patience godliness; and to godliness brotherly kindness; and to brotherly kindness charity.

In verse 5, the apostle Peter instructed us to give *"all diligence"* to a list of items that will affect our attitudes. He went on to say, *"For if these things be in you, and abound, they make you that ye shall neither be barren nor unfruitful in the knowledge of our Lord Jesus Christ"* (verse 8).

It is impossible to have a wrong spirit and think that you can produce a positive IPC. We are instructed to be diligent in developing virtue, knowledge, temperance, patience, godliness, brotherly kindness, and love. When we develop these qualities, we are mirroring the character of God. And doing so will result in positive outcomes in the areas of our lives where we desire to see change.

Conclusion

In our contemporary culture, people seem to be searching for answers to life's issues. However, the truth—God's Word—is, in fact, the answer to all of life's issues. We discussed how volumes have been written, and will continue to be written, addressing the seemingly overwhelming list of human concerns, offering advice and practical steps to mitigate discomfort and minimize injury to the soul. But it is vitally important for us to be able to distinguish genuine truth from "smoke and mirrors."

It is my purpose in writing this book to coach you through life's issues to the end of fulfilling the purpose for which God created you. Each person is a unique expression of God on the earth, and God has placed something in every individual that He thought the world should not be without. Yet many fail to bring forth God's desired expression because of fear, doubt, lack of knowledge, and miscomprehension of God's Word. Establishing and maintaining a relationship with God is vital, for it will dispel these hindrances to fulfilling your God-given purpose.

The path of discovery of your God-given purpose is indeed a journey that can be successfully completed only by following and abiding by the counsel of God's Word and learning to be led continually by the Holy Spirit.

You have only to look at the conditions of the world to realize the importance of your mission and the urgency with which you must soar to purposeful living, thereby living *Life to the Fullest*.

Declaration of Faith for Success

The promises of God will not automatically manifest in your life. You must stand on the Word and become who God says you are.

Some people do not have their priorities in order and would prefer to do any number of things rather than disciplining themselves to read the Bible and study what it says about them, then affirming it by declaring what God says about them.

Faith is expressed ultimately by what you confess and do based on that confession. The conditions of your household, your job, and your relationships depend largely on what you say, which stems from what you believe. You are where you are because of your self-image, which is shaped significantly by the words you continually hear and those you repeatedly speak.

To work toward breaking away from a negative self-image and a fear-filled life, say the confession below. As you continually make this declaration of faith, you will begin to develop faith in all areas of life. Making this confession every day will enable you to stop seeing yourself as a defeated individual who is doomed to failure. Instead, you will see yourself as the world overcomer you are because of how God created you and redeemed you through Christ, filling you with His Spirit.

I have been given authority to become a child of the Most High God. Jesus is made unto me wisdom, righteousness, sanctification, and redemption. Therefore, I confidently say that I am the righteousness of God in Christ. I am more than a conqueror through Jesus. I can do all things through Christ, who strengthens me. For this is the victory that overcomes the world, even my faith, because whatsoever is born of God overcomes the world. I am a world overcomer. In Jesus' name, amen.[1]

Developing a Relationship with God

Wherever I find myself, whether in the local church or on the road, I tell people this truth: Jesus is God's gift to every living human soul on the face of the earth.

It is important to understand our universal and equal need for a Savior. Among His many other titles that tell of His nature, God is known as the Great Physician. Being the author of all life, God knows the optimum conditions necessary to sustain life, the conditions required for creatures to flourish.

After man's disastrous encounter with Satan in the garden of Eden, the Great Physician clearly diagnosed man with a disease of the human spirit—an incurable disease called sin.

Sin's effect on man consists of an inward attitude of rebellion toward God, expressed in outward acts of disobedience. Unfortunately, this disease was passed on to all people as a result of Adam's sin.

The greater issue is that this condition, if not dealt with, is fatal. The stages of development include:

1. Spiritual death, or estrangement from God;

2. The inevitable physical death of the body;

3. The eternal separation from God's presence (the lake of fire and place of eternal torment, biblically called *"the second death"* [Revelation 2:11]).

GOD'S REMEDY FOR SIN

The Lord, as the Great Physician, did not prescribe a mere treatment for our sin; rather, He provided a permanent antidote in the Person of His Son, Jesus Christ, who is our Savior. He doesn't cure our sin—we have it automatically as part of our natural makeups—but He does eliminate its ultimate impact. In fact, He became our sins when He took them to the cross—*"For he hath made him* [Jesus] *to be sin for us, who knew no sin; that we might be made the righteousness of God in him"* (2 Corinthians 5:21, emphasis added).

Jesus came to save us from our sin. Being without sin, He took our sins upon Himself, died in our place, and rose again from the dead so that we might be forgiven and receive eternal life.

> *For the wages of sin is death; but the gift of God is eternal life through Jesus Christ our Lord.* (Romans 6:23)

Indeed, God has provided an eternally effective remedy for all people who will receive it. God loves all people, a truth that John 3:16 affirms: *"For God so loved the world, that he gave his only begotten Son, that whosoever believeth in him should not perish, but have everlasting life."*

Those who accept Jesus as their Savior become righteous, because God has forgiven and forgotten their sins. He says, *"I, even I, am he that blotteth out thy transgressions for mine own sake, and will not remember thy sins"* (Isaiah 43:25). But notice God's attitude toward wickedness, which infects those who hang on to sin and reject God's remedy of salvation: *"The way of the wicked is an abomination unto the Lord: but he loveth him that followeth after righteousness"* (Proverbs 15:9).

So potent is the remedy of God that He provides both eternal life and power to lead a righteous life of victory over sin.

All Must Receive Christ

I have met people who called themselves Christians simply because they had been raised in Christian homes. However, God's offer of salvation, according to Scripture, is to the individual. Salvation must happen on the individual level as a result of personal repentance and acceptance of Christ.

My wife and I have three children. Each of them had to accept God's offer of salvation of his or her own free will; and, praise God, each one did!

Salvation is not based on ethnic background, inheritance, religious rituals, or good works. Salvation comes only through personal faith in Christ's atoning death.

John 1:12 says, *"But as many as received him, to them gave he power to become the sons of God, even to them that believe on his name."*

The Pathway to Eternal Life

To accept God's offer and receive salvation, you must:

1.	*Acknowledge your sinful condition and repent, or turn from sin.*
2.	*Believe that Jesus Christ died for you in order to save you from eternal condemnation.*
3.	*Believe that God raised Jesus from the dead so that you might be justified.*
4.	*Receive the risen Jesus by faith as your personal Savior.*
5.	*Confess Jesus Christ as the Lord of your life.*

Romans 10:9–10 says,

If thou shalt confess with thy mouth the Lord Jesus, and shalt believe in thine heart that God hath raised him from the dead, thou shalt be saved. For with the heart man believeth unto righteousness; and with the mouth confession is made unto salvation.

To receive the salvation that God has provided through the death of His only begotten Son, pray this prayer from your heart:

Dear God,

I come to You, acknowledging that, in my life, I have sinned and have fallen short of Your glory. I repent of all my sins. I confess with my mouth that Jesus Christ, the Son of the living God, died on the cross and shed His blood to save me from my sin. I believe that You raised Jesus from the dead so that I might be justified— just as if I had never sinned. Lord Jesus, come into my heart and live in me now. I make You the Lord of my life. I believe that I receive eternal life through Jesus Christ, my Lord and Savior. I am now made a new creation in Christ, born again of the Spirit of God. In Jesus' name, amen.

If you have prayed this prayer to receive Jesus as your Lord and Savior, tell a friend, family member, or your pastor about it, for *"with the mouth confession is made unto salvation"* (Romans 10:10). Then, please contact us at 770-472-4800 or at victory@bocciusa.org to receive a New Christian Kit.

The Gift of the Holy Spirit

Subsequent to salvation, God has another remarkable, miraculous, and exclusive gift for those who have received Christ into their hearts: He fills them with the Holy Spirit.

The primary purpose of this supernatural experience is to equip you as a believer for effective and authentic testimony to the wonder-working power of God, as well as to enable and facilitate service to advance the kingdom of God.

The Holy Spirit is the Person of the Godhead—which consists of Father, Son, and Holy Spirit—who came to the earth when Jesus returned to heaven. During Jesus' earthly ministry, He could be in only one geographical location at a time. The Holy Spirit, who is omnipresent, assists, manages, and empowers believers to carry out their missions on the earth.

Among other things, the Holy Spirit is also the interpreter, revealer, and illuminator of God's Word to the body of Christ—the church, which encompasses all Christian believers.

When Jesus knew that His mission on earth was nearing its fulfillment, He informed His disciples,

> *But now I go my way to him that sent me....Nevertheless I tell you the truth; it is expedient for you that I go away: for if I go not*

*away, the Comforter will not come unto you; but if I depart, I
will send him unto you.*   (John 16:5, 7)

Christ assured His disciples, both those who walked with Him on
earth and those in this present age, that they would not be left helpless
or hopeless.

SPEAKING IN AN UNKNOWN LANGUAGE

The experience of being filled with the Holy Spirit is like God
Himself ushering you across the threshold and through the gateway of
the supernatural lifestyle that He intended for all who follow Jesus.

It is not a seasonal event, but rather a major part of the lifestyle of faith
that the just, or those who have been declared righteous by God, live by.

So significant is this divine transaction that God has established
an accompanying sign—speaking in tongues—as the initial evidence to
validate the Holy Spirit's indwelling presence in a particular believer.

*And they were all filled with the Holy Ghost, and began to speak
with other tongues, as the Spirit gave them utterance.*
                                                      (Acts 2:4)

A DIVINE POWER SOURCE

*But ye shall receive power, after that the Holy Ghost is come
upon you: and ye shall be witnesses unto me both in Jerusalem,
and in all Judea, and in Samaria, and unto the uttermost part of
the earth.*   (Acts 1:8)

The above passages describe the great purpose of the Holy Spirit's
work and ministry upon believers in the New Testament dispensation.
The Holy Spirit is the power supply from heaven for the body of Christ
at large.

His role in our lives should never be minimized. Jesus certainly
relied upon the Holy Spirit in carrying out His mission. He stands as

the ultimate example of a person entirely dependent upon the power of the Holy Spirit.

If Jesus, the Son of God, needed the Holy Spirit, how much more do we need Him today? Much more! To serve God effectively, we are even more dependent on the Holy Spirit than Jesus was.

BEING FILLED WITH THE HOLY SPIRIT

These are some practical steps you may take to be filled with the Holy Spirit:

1. Be sure you are born again.

If you are a believer, the Holy Spirit has already been involved in your life, helping you to receive Jesus as your Savior and Lord. You are now in a position of readiness to receive His involvement in a much greater way.

2. Simply ask for and receive the Holy Spirit by faith.

The infilling of the Holy Spirit is yours for the asking.

And I say unto you, Ask, and it shall be given you....How much more shall your heavenly Father give the Holy Spirit to them that ask him? (Luke 11:9, 13)

3. Yield to the Holy Spirit.

Expect what the Scripture says will happen to those who are filled with the Holy Spirit. When you speak of your own free will, you will discover the supernatural provision of dialogue. The Holy Spirit will not take over your mouth. You must do the speaking.

Here is an appropriate prayer to receive the infilling of the Holy Spirit:

Heavenly Father,

I thank You that I am Your very own child, and I thank You for making available to me the outpouring of Your Holy Spirit.

I now ask You to fill me with Your Holy Spirit so that I may be effective in witness and service to You for the glory of Your kingdom. I fully expect the accompanying evidence of speaking with other tongues. I yield myself to Your Spirit now, in the name of Jesus. Amen.

If you have prayed this prayer to be filled with the Holy Spirit, please contact us at 770-472-4800 or at victory@bocciusa.org to receive a New Christian Kit.

Endnotes

Introduction

[1]"Commentary on Genesis 3," *Commentary Critical and Explanatory on the Whole Bible*, Robert Jamieson, D.D., available from http://bible.crosswalk.com/Commentaries/JamiesonFaussetBrown/jfb.cgi?book=ge&chapter=003, s.v. "Genesis 3:6–9," verse 8.

[2]See the explanation for praying in the Spirit/speaking in tongues in the section of this book entitled "Developing a Relationship with God."

Chapter 1

[1]Jesus is the second Person of the Godhead (Father, Son, and Holy Spirit); He is God in the flesh: *"In [Jesus] the whole fullness of Deity (the Godhead) continues to dwell in bodily form [giving complete expression of the divine nature]"* (Colossians 2:9 AMP).

[2]Based on information from *The KJV Strong's Version*, available from http://www.studylight.org/desk/?query=Genesis+1%3A28&translation=str, #8762, s.v. "blessed," Genesis 1:28.

[3]Based on information from "Hebrew Lexicon entry for Shama," *The KJV Old Testament Hebrew Lexicon*, by ed. Brown, Driver, Briggs, and Gesenius, available from http://www.biblestudytools.net/Lexicons/Hebrew/heb.cgi?number=8085&version=kjv, s.v. "hearken diligently," Deuteronomy 28:1.

Chapter 3

[1]*Merriam-Webster's Collegiate Dictionary*, 11th ed., s.v. "offense."

Chapter 4

[1]*Merriam-Webster's Collegiate Dictionary*, 11th ed., s.v. "esteem."

[2]Ibid.

CHAPTER 6

[1]Based on information from "Hebrew Lexicon entry for Sakal," *The KJV Old Testament Hebrew Lexicon*, Brown, Driver, Briggs, and Gesenius, http://www.biblestudytools.net/Lexicons/Hebrew/heb. cgi?number=7919&version=kjv, s.v. "success," Joshua 1:8.

[2]Based on information from "Hebrew Lexicon entry for Yakach," Brown, Driver, Briggs, and Gesenius, available from http://www.biblestudytools.net/Lexicons/Hebrew/heb. cgi?number=3198&version=kjv, s.v. "together," Isaiah 1:18.

CHAPTER 7

[1]"Greek Lexicon entry for Metanoeo," *The KJV New Testament Greek Lexicon*, by ed. Thayer and Smith, available from http://www.biblestudytools.net/Lexicons/Greek/grk. cgi?number=3340&version=kjv, s.v. "repent," Matthew 4:17.

DECLARATION OF FAITH FOR SUCCESS

[1]Scripture references for this faith confession are, respectively: 1 John 3:1; 1 Corinthians 1:30; 2 Corinthians 5:21; Romans 8:37; Philippians 4:13; 1 John 5:4.

About the Author

Dr. Joseph M. Ripley Sr. is founder and pastor of the Body of Christ Church International, USA, a nondenominational church with two locations in the State of Georgia: Alpharetta and College Park. What began in 1983 with fifty people is now a thriving ministry to several thousand congregants.

The Body of Christ Church International, USA, has multifaceted outreach programs that minister in schools, prisons, youth detention centers, and cities, both domestic and abroad. The church sponsors Success in Life classes, healing school, soulwinning training, I.M.P.A.C.T. tutorial program, Business by the Book, and Big Brother/Big Sister, in addition to others. The ministry also operates a Technology Learning Center, which reaches the world for Jesus through technology. It provides computer classes and associated teaching and training.

Dr. Ripley is an internationally known author and motivational conference speaker, having traveled to such extreme global corners as Hawaii, Central America, Australia, Africa, and China. His show, *Living in Victory*, is broadcast worldwide on television channels, radio stations, and the Internet. Through this outreach, Dr. Ripley teaches believers to "feed their faith and starve their doubts to death." He is also a life coach to celebrities, entertainers, athletes, and other high-profile people.

A graduate of the Valley Forge Military Academy in Wayne, Pennsylvania, Dr. Ripley also attended the University of Georgia, where he majored in broadcast journalism and political science. He holds a doctoral degree from the New Covenant International Bible College in Auckland, New Zealand.

Dr. Ripley and his wife, Dr. Marjanita L. Ripley, are the proud parents of three children: April, Heather, and Joseph Jr.

To learn more about the Body of Christ Church International, USA, visit www.bocciusa.org or send an e-mail to victory@bocciusa.org.

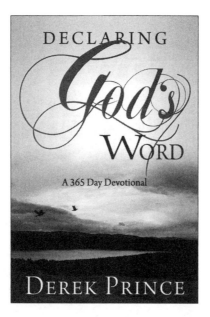

Declaring God's Word: A 365-Day Devotional
Derek Prince

According to Scripture, Satan can be defeated if believers will stand on God's Word and testify to what it says about the mighty and powerful blood of Jesus—blood that cleanses us from sin and makes us righteous. For the first time, acclaimed Bible teacher Derek Prince will lead you to power and victory in this yearlong daily devotional. By *Declaring God's Word*, you will become steeped in the Scriptures and overcome satanic oppression and attacks. Begin each new day by confessing the truth of God's Word, and you will experience the love, power, and wisdom of God all year long.

ISBN: 978-1-60374-067-8 ✦ Trade ✦ 432 pages

WHITAKER
HOUSE

The Principles and Power of Vision
Dr. Myles Munroe

Whether you are a businessperson, a homemaker, a student, or a head of state, author Myles Munroe explains how you can make your dreams and hopes a living reality. Your success is not dependent on the state of the economy or what the job market is like. You do not need to be hindered by the limited perceptions of others or by a lack of resources. Discover time-tested principles that will enable you to fulfill your vision no matter who you are or where you come from. You were not meant for a mundane or mediocre life. You do not exist just to earn a paycheck. Revive your passion for living. Pursue your dream. Discover your vision—and find your true life.

ISBN: 978-0-88368-951-6 ✦ Hardcover ✦ 240 pages

WHITAKER
HOUSE

Get Up, Get Out, Get Blessed
Bryan Cutshall

Israel's triumphant journey out of slavery in Egypt and into the Promised Land of Canaan can quickly be your victory in life. Author Bryan Cutshall brilliantly unpacks this incredible story of deliverance, wandering, and promise and applies it to your life today so that you may live a life of triumph and blessings, stop stress from affecting your life, overcome fear and mediocrity, and eliminate doubt and bitterness. *Get Up, Get Out, Get Blessed* will lead you into the miraculous life of power God has planned for you.

ISBN: 978-1-60374-054-8 • Trade • 272 pages

WHITAKER
HOUSE

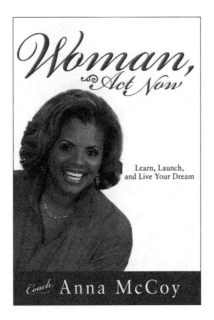

Woman, Act Now
Anna McCoy

Experience personal and business success greater than you ever imagined possible. Anna McCoy is powerfully anointed to help you find and walk out your divine destiny. She will inspire and encourage you to fulfill your personal vision, break free from financial hindrances, and identify and develop your hidden gifts. Overcome negative criticism and defeat self-doubt and fear as you reach your potential as a woman of God. Act now and execute your dreams!

ISBN: 978-1-60374-068-5 • Hardcover • 304 pages

WHITAKER
HOUSE

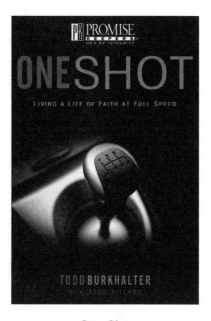

One Shot
Todd Burkhalter

Yⁿou have one shot at this life. One shot to make it count. If
you don't make the most of it, you risk wasting your life.
What story will your life tell? God designed your life to be lived
with purpose, passion, and direction. Your life was intended
to mean something. In *One Shot*, author Todd Burkhalter
challenges men to live a life of adventure and significance. True
risk always begins in the heart. By understanding who we are
in Jesus Christ and who He is in us, you can experience the
adventure, meet life's challenges, and live a significant life of
faith at full speed.

ISBN: 978-1-60374-071-5 ♦ Trade ♦ 208 pages

WHITAKER
HOUSE

Right People, Right Place, Right Plan
Jentezen Franklin

Whom should I marry? What will I do with my life? Do I take this job? Should I invest money in this opportunity? God has bestowed an incredible gift in the heart of every believer. He has given you an internal compass to help guide your life, your family, your children, your finances, and much more. Jentezen Franklin reveals how, through the Holy Spirit, you can tap into the heart and mind of the Almighty. Learn to trust those divine "nudges" and separate God's voice from all other voices in your life. Tap into your supernatural gift of spiritual discernment and you will better be able to fulfill your purpose as a child of God.

ISBN: 978-0-88368-276-0 ♦ Hardcover ♦ 208 pages

WHITAKER
HOUSE